WHAT DARKNESS REMAINS

NEXUS OF NIGHTMARES
BOOK 3

NICHOLAS BARKER

HANGAR 1 PUBLISHING

1

"Mr. Dorsett, could you please concentrate on our conversation?" the agent asked.

"How do you expect me to concentrate when you ask me just the right questions to bring back lost memories of that place?" Mr. Dorsett asked.

"The point of meeting with you is to hear your story, but you must give me the information in a prompt manner. Otherwise, we will be here all night".

"Let me be clear then. What happened to my family and I is nothing short of a tragedy, and I will not let that go under any circumstances. Just because you need to document everything for your file... you set this meeting, and I will take the time that I need".

"That is acceptable, Mr. Dorsett, but I will have to hold several interviews with you. I don't mind, but I am rather busy".

"Then go there yourself and investigate".

"We are not holding such an investigation just yet. Now, please start over, and I will try to follow you".

"Well...I believe everything began in June of 1993. Jeanette and I had just begun looking for another home."

"Please state who Jeanette would be to you."

"Jeanette is my ex-wife. Now, may I continue?"

"Yes, but please be specific on each person. We have to keep this straight for the file."

Mr. Dorsett rolled his eyes then stared into his coffee again as the memories flooded his mind. Jeanette and I argued for weeks about what area we would move to next. The company had...sorry, CSX demanded that we move to West Virginia for my work.

It wasn't a problem, except that Jeanette and I argued about which area to move into for about three weeks. I don't remember what town she chose anymore, but I can tell you that it was closer to the city.

Eventually, we settled on the idea of moving into the Fairmont area of West Virginia. It wasn't the most ideal setting for our family, but it was close to the depot in Clarksburg. That was the most important to me, but she wanted something beautiful. We had heard that the area was beautiful beyond belief, but I still feared living away from a major city. It was a hell of a move from Richmond to some small town we had never heard of in a state that seemed remote in every direction.

Our youngest daughter, Brianna, seemed to be the most resistant to leaving our home in Richmond, even though she had not started school yet or made many friends. Though I could understand, it was all she had ever known about living anywhere. However, her mother had convinced her that this would be the best for all of us. I knew she still felt different about it than the rest of us. Although Nicole and Eric didn't voice their opinion, they would rather have remained in Richmond with their friends. Yet none of us had a choice in the matter when it came to earning money or not.

The matter fell upon me to resolve as I had taken two weeks off from work to find a place to live in Fairmont. We packed our things and began selling our home through a local realtor, then drove from Richmond to Fairmont on June 7th. That morning held no events other than packing everyone into the car before sunrise. We made great time as we pulled into Harrisonburg, VA, around seven in the morning. It wasn't the best area to stop in, but we had food to eat and could stretch our legs for a few moments.

I think we pulled into a place called L&S Diner on Liberty Street. It was a nice place and very quaint for a quick family breakfast before hitting the road again. I don't remember what we had eaten, but it was delicious. The coffee was excellent for such a small place."

"Mr. Dorsett, please focus."

"Right...we pulled out of the diner only to stop for gas and some snacks. I had decided that we would not stop again until we reached Fairmont, if possible. I couldn't stop my mind from feeling a sense of unease as we neared our destination, but I just shook it off and pushed on. I remember coming over a hill and seeing the whole town before us. It was a sight to behold for sure, but the mountains seemed foreboding at that moment.

We pulled into town and immediately went to the realtor's office. I don't remember the place's name, but the realtor was odd, to say the least. She seemed preoccupied with us staying within the city, but we had other plans. I remember Jeanette and I arguing with her for ten minutes about the areas we wanted to check out. Fuck...that was an interesting day, to say the least. Eventually, she relented, and we packed ourselves into the car once again to head to the hotel.

Life was different back then as you couldn't search for things online like you could today. Sure, places had the internet, but it wasn't as reliable in the country as it was in Richmond. So we had to let the lady know what areas we wanted and then give her a day or two to look at her listings. I do remember that she had several homes that had become available to sell. Though we didn't wish to stay in a shitty motel, we didn't have much of a choice.

We checked into the Super 8 just off Landing Lane in Fairmont and got into our room around 1 pm that day. It wasn't hard to settle in for the night hoping to find our home the next day. The rest of the evening was a blur, but we walked down to the Cracker Barrel near the motel. The kids bitched about the trip and staying in a motel, but we had to remind them that it was hard on all of us. After our meal, Jeanette took the kids back to the motel to get ready for bed for the night, and I went to use the payphone outside the motel."

"Who did you call?"

"I called my sister back in Richmond and told her we had arrived safely. She was the only family that I had left. I didn't like her much nor did we connect at all, but she was family, which was what mattered at the time. She was happy to hear that we had made it to Fairmont safely. Then she said something that I will never forget, at least I think it was her that said it. "I won't make it to your next birthday" and "beware her stare".

I was confused, but I shrugged it off and cut the call short. I wasn't sure if anyone had been listening to our call and just spoke in those moments, but she swore that she never heard anything like that or said that when I called her next. Though the voice was right. I put the phone back on the hanger and lit a cigarette. I remember standing there and hearing the sounds of the city around me. These sounds bled into the whistling of birds and the low roar of air washing over the mountains.

I felt alone and depressed at that moment, but I could not understand why. I mean...I had everything! I had a great family with a supportive wife. I had a new position that paid a lot of money, and I seemed happy, but it was as though something had taken over me and sucked all the joy away. I didn't contemplate it too much, however, as I slowly and methodically smoked my cigarette and took in the world around me. I remember thinking about how out of place it was that I would move away from the city in which I was born, but it was ok. My family and I would have a fresh start in this amazing place, and I would be able to give them whatever they wanted.

The heat outside didn't bother me, but it was a slow build to the middle of the summer that year. I never understood how a place could be that far north and still hold humidity. I didn't think to question it then as I was glad to be ending our move soon.

I walked back to our room without anything else happening until the next morning. I had set the alarm clock that night, and I knew that it was working, but it didn't go off the next morning. It was plugged into the wall and should have sounded right away at 6 am, but it didn't. The thing that woke us all was the sound of the desk ringing into the room. It was the realtor calling for us around 10 am.

We all jumped up and threw our clothes on to meet her. She had given us an address, but it was on a road a little away from the motel. I remember that address like no other: 766 Middletown Road. The address rolled right off the tongue, as I remember, but it would eventually come to haunt our dreams."

"Mr. Dorsett, your hands are shaking. Are you alright?"

"Yeah...I'm fine, but I don't like thinking about this at all."

"Then let's get through this as quickly as we can."

"We left as quickly as we could and journeyed through he countryside to that address. I knew that there had to be other homes that were more suitable, but that place was different. I can't quite understand it all, but it was a place that attracted Jeanette and the kids immediately. It was a quaint little place just over the river and atop a hill. The house faced away from the road, which left the rest of the ridge as a back yard. The remainder of the hillside was forest, with the main road just below.

I should have known what would happen with love at first sight, but how was I to know?"

"Mr. Dorsett, you're shaking again."

Mr. Dorsett took in a deep breath and then exhaled. He held out a Camel cigarette in his hand. "Do you mind?"

"Not in the least. If it will calm your nerves."

He flicked his lighter quickly and placed the cig in his mouth. With a few puffs, the cigarette burned brightly in the dimly lit room.

"We drove up to the house and began looking around until the realtor arrived. I remember yelling at the kids to stay near Jeanette and me until we could get into the home. They were so excited and ran about in the yard for a moment. The sun beat down on us, leaving those little green streaks on my vision until I could get my shades back on from wiping them. I walked about for a moment and checked out the outside of the home. I noticed windows for a basement, but I could not see into them at all. Cobwebs were all over the windows and hung down to the ground on one side.

I remember seeing something moving inside the basement as I

stood there, drawing me in. I was so intently trying to see what it was that I didn't notice Jeanette approaching me from my right.

"What are you looking at?" She asked quickly.

I jumped back as I yelled, "Jesus, fuck!".

"Sorry about that, honey. What are you looking at?"

I looked back, but I couldn't see anything moving. Naturally, I smiled and said nothing. Jeanette stared at me for a moment, then said, "The realtor has arrived. She said she is ready to show us the house."

"Ok, I'm coming."

I followed Jeanette around the house until we met with the realtor. She didn't go anywhere near the house, however. She just handed me the key and said, "Have fun!".

So...we entered the house and began looking around. It was a beautiful old house and looked like it was built at the turn of the century. However, I don't really know much about houses or architecture. The floors creaked with each step, but they were solid enough. I don't know how long the house had been on the market, but it seemed stale on the inside. Jeanette rushed the kids to the second floor to look at the rooms. I was more interested in looking around the dining room and kitchen. I didn't see any water damage or leaks, so it was good enough for me.

I even checked the cabinet under the sink and didn't smell mildew or any moisture rotting the wood. There was a pantry off the kitchen and a living room that seemed arranged long ways to the rest of the downstairs rooms. It was a nice size, though, with a fireplace that divided the room in half. I also thought that it was odd that this room alone had three windows, but the kitchen had one, and the dining room had two. It was as though they increased the amount of windows by one as they were building the bottom floor of the house.

I then looked at the hallway again and found the door to the basement, but it seemed sealed from the inside. I should have broken into it, with what I know now, but I wasn't sure we would purchase the home then."

Mr. Dorsett took a long drag from his cigarette and then breathed our as he rubbed his forehead. As he began to speak again, he rolled up the sleeves of his dress shirt and unbuttoned his collar.

"At first, I thought that the realtor was just odd, but when I walked out to talk with her about the house, she was sitting in her car just staring at the front of the house. I walked about half way to her, then turned and looked up to see what she was looking at, but I only saw the kids moving the curtains around in a room on the second level. I shook my head and walked up to the window without her reacting. One knock on the glass, and she jumped. I don't know how she didn't notice me coming right at her, but she didn't.

She rolled the window down and laughed nervously as she addressed me. "I am sorry, Mr. Dorsett. I must have drifted off into a day dream. How do you like the house?"

"I like it alright, but what is up with the basement door being sealed?"

She looked back toward the front door again and stammered.

"I...I don't know...uhh...I was told to let you look around the house by yourself and allow you to take it all in. I don't know much about the house, and I have never been inside it. Ummm, my boss was the one that checked the place out, so..."

She smiled nervously and then brushed the hair from over her left eye.

"How can you sell a house that you have never been in? And why would you just let us go in without a guided showing? Is something wrong with this house?"

My questions seemed to fall upon deaf ears as she just stared at the front of the house again. I also gazed at the front of the house in that moment, but I couldn't see anything. The whole house had been painted a rustic white color, but I could tell it was originally just brown boards that had been treated. The roof seemed to have been in good shape from where I was standing, but I don't really know much about roofs either.

Old, white curtains hung in the windows and seemed to move about slightly like the air had switched on. The other odd thing is that two windows were visible on the bottom right of the front of the home, but none on the left. The two windows for the dinning room to the left of the doorway seemed to have been moved to the other wall at some point. The top windows were three in a row beside each other, with the middle window framed above the door.

I thought this was an odd design choice, but I didn't consider it too much. I looked at the realtor again, but she had not moved her gaze from the home for the time I had been there. I walked back to the door only to notice that there had been some heavy locks inside the door at one point, but they were only shadows in the wood now. The back door down the hall from the front door seemed to have the same, but the locks were still in place there.

This piqued my interest as I could not understand why anyone would have heavy locks on one door and not the other. The rest of the house seemed to be normal, except the windows on the bottom floor had been nailed shut. The beautiful wood stairs wrapped upward to the second floor with rooms starting from my left and going around to the right side of the home. A bathroom had been built without an exterior window and was positioned above the dining room and kitchen. This all seemed normal, and no damage could be seen still.

This was when Jeanette and the kids emerged from different rooms only to stand before me and ask, "Can we live here, dad?". Every one of them seemed to have aligned against me on the matter as I wished to see more homes, but they all wanted this one. The only thing that made me relent was the fact that it was close to I-79 for me to head to work in Clarksburg. That...and Brianna gave me the puppy eyes as she stood there in a little red dress, clutched her teddy bear, and said, "Daddy, I would love this house, and I have picked out my room already. Please can we stay here?"

Who was I to deny my family when they had united in one idea for the first time in history? This was a rare occurrence, and I would never get such cooperation from children again. So we purchased the home and moved in two days after looking it over. The odd thing is that the realtor met us as we left the motel and handed us the keys. She had never dared to go back to that house the whole time we signed the papers or anything else. I worried that the keys weren't event the correct ones, but that fear was dashed on moving day when we unlocked the house without issue.

The moving truck arrived and backed near the door. Burly movers jumped from the cab and began unloading everything into the house. Jeanette started in the kitchen and began unpacking the boxes as they arrived. It was hot as hell that day, and I just remember sweat dripping from my brow the whole time we were moving the stuff in. The kids were in their respective rooms and began unpacking everything dropped outside their doors. Everything about that move went too smoothly, which made me happy, but I still thought it was odd. As I remember, the movers left our property around seven o'clock, and all of our stuff had been put into place. Even our heavy-ass TV set on its stand seemed to be just right within the space. Then I jumped in the station wagon and hit the road to the nearest store for some groceries. I had to spend the last amount of cash to get food, but it would all pay off. My check would be sent to the Clarksburg office soon for me to pick it up and cash it.

I drove along the roads as they wound through to the countryside back into Fairmont. The whole area was amazing, and the mountains stood in stark contrast to the world I had left behind. I began to light another cigarette as I approached the grocery store we had pointed out when we first looked at the house. It was a few moments before I went inside, and as I finished my cigarette in the car. Everything seemed normal until I could feel that someone was staring at me. I looked all around the area, but I saw no one. Especially no one who was looking at me. So I shrugged it off, stepped out of the wagon, and threw my cigarette on the ground. I don't really remember what I had bought, but I do remember that it came out to 66.70 because the girl put ten cents of her own money into it, so the total wasn't 66.60.

Seeing her doing that was humorous to me at the time as I was not a superstitious man. However I didn't judge her as some would because she was a superstitious person and a small-town world. She would have viewed the are as the city, but as someone who had originally lived in Atlanta, it was a small town. I grabbed the groceries and returned to the house as quickly as possible. I remember arriving to see Jeanette sitting outside with the kids and remarking on the heat of the day. I just had to hold out a Red Baron Pepperoni Pizza for the kids to start screaming and running into the house again. I could immediately feel that the air had not been on for some time as the house was humid even at night.

I placed the groceries on the counter and hurried the kids back into the yard to play. Jeanette put the groceries away as I prepared the oven to have some well-earned pizza. She then approached me and said, "I think the air conditioning is broken. It runs some but then stops like it's overheating. I sighed and began looking around the house for any indication of a breaker box. I saw nothing until I passed the door to the basement again. I could feel that my mind had been made up that the basement would be out salvation to get the air running again. So I did what any father would do and kicked the door in. It took a couple tries, but I got the bastard open.

As I stood in the doorway, I could smell this odd scent. It wasn't like a rotting smell or a wet smell but like a tomb. The air was cold and seemed heavy as I slowly worked my way down the decrepit wooden stairs and into the basement proper. Immediately, I felt uneasy as though I had walked into and awkward situation. However, I did see the breaker box on the far wall, so I helped myself. It didn't take long to see that the breaker had flipped to the air, so I flipped it on and waited for a moment. Just then, a rumble moved through the house all around the basement as the air conditioning roared to life. I don't know what that sound was, but it freaked me out."

Mr. Dorsett rubbed his forehead again, then stretched his arm toward the ashtray.

"Please continue with your account"

"I'm sorry, but why the fuck do I have to retell this? We have been over this story twice already."

"Mr. Dorsett, do you think it is prudent to stop here and pick up tomorrow?"

"I think it's ok to continue, but my mind has begun to block some memories."

"Take a break, and we will continue in ten minutes if you wish."

The agent signaled something to the only window in the room as the door was unlocked.

"Get some air, Mr. Dorsett. We will continue in a moment."

John did as the agent said and walked outside an auxiliary door to get some air in the alley. He did not understand why he had been brought in to recount his story again or who these people were, but cooperating was the best thing in his mind. The year was 2001, and everything seemed to different from the time his story had been set within. He pulled hard on his cigarette as if it would bring relief from this situation. How could the world have moved forward so quickly only to be left a zombie of the decade before?

The sounds of New York City seemed to be loud at this moment as his mind refused to focus on the world around him. He was now stuck in 1993 mentally and had no time to process the world. Every drag from his cigarette came with a flood of memories about the family that had been lost to the history of his life. Jeanette was no longer a fixture in this broken man's life, and he struggled to come to terms with that reality. The air that was supposed to calm his tortured psyche now seemed to damn him more and more. Eventually, the door behind him had been unlocked and opened to allow him inside the building again. The chance to run had faded, but he wouldn't dream of it with these "agents" around.

John entered the room again and took his seat. He immediately sniffed out his cigarette, only to pull another and light it. The agent smiled as he did this and then motioned for him to resume. The world seemed to fade as John entered his past again.

The pizza was really good, and the evening going into that night seemed like any other. We played Uno in the living room until the kids' bedtime. I told them all good night and kissed them on their heads, and then Jeanette marched them off to their beds. My first instinct was to lock that basement up by putting a bookshelf so that the door could not open at all. Then I locked the back door. I went out onto the front porch to smoke only for Jeanette to emerge from the house behind me.

"This place is gorgeous, baby. The kids love their new rooms and all the space that we have here."

"I'm glad it's everything that you guys wanted."

"You don't like the house?"

"It's not that, just a lot to get done to be settled in. I'm just hoping nothing goes wrong."

Jeanette sighed andmuttered, "typical".

"I'll like the home soon enough."

That seemed to be enough for her as she took a cigarette from the soft pack . I stared at her for a moment as I continued to smoke my cigarette. "I think this will be a great start for all of us, babe."

She stared back at me for a moment, then kissed me.

John sat in silence for a moment as he took another drag. He fought back the tears that welled inside his throat. That was the most magical night I have had my whole life. Our marriage had been stale for some time and I knew she wanted to be done with it all, but that moment showed me she still cared enough for us to hang around. She had always accused me of hiding something or not allowing her in, but I never figured out why that was.

We sat there and smoked as we watched the sun slowly dip behind the mountains in the distance. The silence was deafening as we continued to sit until she stood and went back into the house. I finished my cigarette and threw it into the yard before moving to the door. In the darkness, I could feel something behind me toward the woods as I heard a rustling of the plants. Just then, a breeze blew through the area and I turned to see nothing. I just went inside and locked the door before falling asleep in the living room.

Jeanette had slept alone for some time, and I could not understand why she would not have me in our bed. That was my last thought before I fell asleep. How can I be surrounded by my family and be so isolated?

John sat back in his chair as he put the last of his cigarette out in the ashtray.

2

"Tell me about the next day that you can remember."

"I think several days passed after that night. I had taken to sleeping in the living room continuously as I never felt comfortable sleeping on the upper floors. Though I was sure it was a quirk I had developed rather than a deeper fear. When I was up there alone, however, I felt like I was being watched. It wasn't from the house around me but more like someone was watching me through the windows. I felt it everywhere, even when not near a window at all.

It was a Friday, I think, when that goddamned breaker went out again, and the air conditioning shut off. Naturally, I had no money to seek out an electrician, but it was an easy fix. Just turn the breaker off and switch it back on after the load had been taken off the unit. I even opened the side wall that led into the pantry and checked the central unit, but I found nothing. I knew there had to be short, but I was not willing to tear into the walls to find it. So I continued to fuck with that breaker again until the world fell silent. It was strange because I remember everything making noise like a minute before. Now, it was like someone turned the sounds off completely.

The already tense air seemed to become heavier. The kids were with Jeanette in town, leaving me at home to finish reviewing the electrical systems. I flipped another breaker off, then on. In the moment between sounds, I paused only to hear slow and lumbering footsteps moving from the dining room into the hall and stopping at the door to the basement. I rushed upstairs to see if Jeanette had returned, but she hadn't. Though the door stood open and waved back and forth in the wind blowing into the home.

Immediately, I noticed that the sounds had now been turned back on, for lack of a better term. I saw no one but checked the house to make sure. I shrugged my shoulders as I looked out the front window. I could see Jeanette and the kids coming up the driveway to our home. That was the first time I had been alone in the home, which was interesting. I don't know who or what it was that would have opened the door and walked across the house, but I relegated it to the house being really old.

Jeanette and the kids had brought food for me from McDonald's, and I could not resist as it was the only meal I had had that day. Jeanette instantly recognized that something was off, but I simply whispered that something odd happened. I also stated that I thought it was simply the house settling, but she asked for the details anyway. Upon telling her such, she looked about the dining room and peered into the kitchen. As I had noticed some moments before, nothing seemed out of place. She shrugged it off as I had done, and we concluded our night with board games. On this night, however, she asked me to bed with her, but I could feel she was using me for comfort.

I didn't care a bit since it was better to sleep in the bed than on the couch. I remember nothing else from that night other than having a dream about Jeanette, but it was the usual incoherent dream.

Look...the further I go in this story, the more I want to stop. You cannot expect me to call up memories so damaging to me as a person and a man. I lost my family to this shit!"

"We must study this incident for our own records."

"I don't even know who you people are, and I certainly don't need to place some organization that documents people's pain."

"This must be done, and if you cannot cooperate, we can visit your home relentlessly until we get the information."

The agent sat back in his seat and stared across the table at John Dorsett.

"Very well, but I need some more cigs. You have any?"

The agent wasted no time producing a pack of Marlboro's from his shirt pocket. The odd thing was that the seal had not been broken.

"Who in the fuck carries around an untouched pack of cigarettes?"

"You need not worry about that, but to be thankful that I had cigarettes for you to smoke. I can provide such things in exchange for cooperation."

"You guys are pricks, but you got me by the balls here."

"Then let's continue with the next day that you remember."

"And what if that is all that I remember?"

"Then we move to phase 2, and we extract what we can under hypnosis."

John looked down at his coffee again as he lit another cigarette. After that, he swallowed a swig of the black liquid and revisited the memories again.

"Nothing really happened on the weekends. We were either not home most of the day, or things just seemed to be calm. I don't know why or how, but that is how it was. I just know that Mondays were odd until 7 o'clock, then went to a different place by 12 AM.

The following Monday, from my last memory, was the start of the last week that I would be out of work so naturally, I am home alone a lot. I just remember climbing to the roof and inspecting the fireplace for signs that it had been blocked or infested. Bats weren't uncommon in this area, from what the realtor had indicated, so we needed to be cautious. I remember shining the light into the chimney and looking about before seeing something moving in the dim light.

Just on the edge of the light from the flashlight, I could see something moving about, but it didn't seem like a bat or small animal. I don't really know how to describe it to you, but it was off-putting. It looked like a child inside the chimney that was folding and unfolding itself. I wasn't scared but creeped out. When I looked away and looked again, it was a bird that had begun flopping about in the chimney, but with a thud, it fell into the living room.

I was sure that my mind was collapsing under the stress of a failing marriage. I don't know if you guys have kids, but it crushes you as a man to watch your wife being happy away from you. Your dreams are filled with ways to solve the issue, and you seem to wish she hadn't checked out. I knew something more serious was happening, but she never wanted to talk about it. I can't force her, so what am I to do except be a good dad for my children. Though the sense of failure is overwhelming at times.

It took some time for me to gather my thoughts on that roof, so I just remember sitting beside the chimney and smoking a cigarette before moving down the ladder again. The air was stirring a lot, and the day had been much cooler than the days before. It might have been June, but it felt more like May with all the wind flowing about. The trees brushed about in the air and made the normal rustling sound, like someone spreading hay on a field.

I must have sat there for thirty minutes until I could hear a car approaching from the bottom of the driveway, so I climbed down and investigated. I stood at the front of the house and watched as someone drove up the driveway and turned around, but while they did this, they just stared at me. It was the oddest thing because my eyes were locked on their face and nothing else. I don't remember seeing anything but them staring at me. It was an older man with those old eighties frames, and he just stared at me intently before driving away.

I thought that was fucking odd, but I related it to the embarrassment of being seen in a stranger's driveway. After he drove away, I just went into the house and looked for that bird. It was dead on the floor just in front of the fireplace, as I had suspected that it would be, so I cleaned it up and threw the body outside. Since that was my only task for the day, I cracked a Budweiser open and turned on the TV. It was frustrating to have to stand hunched over in the living room and click the dials until I could see an image, but I did it.

I watched reruns of My Favorite Martian and sipped the beer until the world seemed to fade away. It was either that or break out the Atari and attempt to beat the empire in The Empire Strikes Back. That shit wasn't going to happen, though. After dealing with such serious thoughts, I was in no mood to be challenged by pixels on the screen. Jeanette and the kids would arrive home around five so I had a lot of time. I thought about investigating the upper floors further to check for any plumbing issues or rooms that weren't being used.

I finished my beer and moved over to the bottom of the stairs, only to stand there and peer up to the second floor. Something seemed to be stopping me from climbing the stairs at that moment. I don't know what it was, but I felt exposed by being there like a sniper having to move spots in a firefight. I wanted to duck for cover and hide from this house, but I resisted. I was a man, goddammit, and I was not going to allow this house to beat me. I pushed this feeling off as just being paranoid and depressed from my current family situation.

I climbed the stairs slowly until I reached the top and began looking about. Everything seemed quiet and peaceful at that moment, so I began looking into each of the rooms. I remember seeing the kid's rooms and smiling at all the toys across the floor. Especially with Eric having his transformer toys standing on the floor as if preparing to defend earth from Megatron. I laughed about this for a few minutes until I could feel the warmth.

I left that doorway and moved to Jeanette's room, but I could see something inside. I don't know what it was, but in the crack of the door, I could see what looked like her kissing another man as he slid his hands down her body. The thought crippled me, and I crumpled to the floor in the hallway. I don't know how that sight had come to be as I knew her to never be the type to cheat, but it seemed like something the house wanted me to see."

A tear began to form on Mr. Dorsett's cheek and flow down as he sniffled.

"She was all that I had, and I could never have wished for her to do such things, but my mind would not let me unsee that. I know that

I lay on the floor and cried for twenty minutes. I found that I was propped up by the wall and was sitting looking into her room. I knew that she had removed herself from me a year before, and she had been wishing to be free of our marriage. It wasn't that she said that, but more like the understanding that this was the case.

At that moment, I died a little inside and stopped caring that she would do something like that. It was the only way to preserve my mind and force myself to continue forward. I had often thought, however, that I may not have been the man she wished to obtain in life, so she resisted our love. It left my heart broken nonetheless, but I could not show this in front of the children, and I had to be strong to bring us all together. I can't say why I thought that, but I did.

After a moment more, I stood from the floor and dried my eyes only to enter her room and look around. Nothing seemed odd or to indicate that the vision I had witnessed moments before was correct. Though I did feel a tension and irritation that I would not have felt otherwise. I don't know what it was, but it seemed like I was feeling how Jeanette felt. I can't explain that so I'll move on.

The rest of the evening was normal, and I could find no issues with the house either on the lower or upper levels. I did see that the pantry had a loose board, so I hammered that back in until I could replace the old wood. Otherwise, I went back to drinking beer and watching TV. Jeanette didn't like me to smoke in the house with the kids home, but I could when alone, so I lit up. The jeans and red flannel shirt I wore were worse for wear as I had been working around the house most of that morning.

I had explored the crawl spaces under the house that branched from the basement, so I was dirty. I made sure to knock most of it off outside the home, though. The Camels tasted so good when paired with a nice Budweiser and a Nick at Nite rerun marathon. I thought it was odd that this would be on late in the evening, around 4 or so, but I watched anyway. I only turned it off after I rolled a joint and stepped outside. The taste of the weed was nice on my lips, even though I still could taste the beer as well. I entertained myself, however, by lighting another cigarette and smoking both at the same time.

I thought that everything was cool until everyone showed up at around six. The day was coming to a close, but slowly, as the summer sun refused to give up its vigil. Though faded, the light did for a moment. I scratched out my cigarette and walked around the house to meet my family again.

"Hey, baby! How was your day at home?"

"It was good but fruitless. Nothing seems to be wrong with the house, which I find odd in an old structure like this. I even crawled around under the house looking for damage but found nothing. How was the swimming lessons?"

Brianna had indicated that she loves learning to swim, while Nicole and Eric couldn't care less. Jeanette had enjoyed her day of shopping for things that we needed in the house. She even visited Walmart for some cleaning supplies that we desperately needed. She was determined to clean the house from top to bottom before I returned to work. It was then that I realized my thoughts of going to work caused a slight rise in stress for some reason. I don't know why as I knew the job inside and out until it had become a second thought to do the work.

Perhaps it was that I feared my family would fragment with me leaving the home for most of the day. Jeanette worked a part-time job before but was actively working to find something in Fairmont. I was sure she would find something by the end of the week if she had been looking hard enough. It was nice for her to be available for the kids, as I could not be while working 25 minutes away in Clarksburg.

I helped Jeanette into the house with the stuff she had bought and set it all in the hallway until we could find a better place. She was the one with the decorating vision, so I trusted her. All I knew to do was take the kids into the yard and play football until the sun went down. That night, we all settled on the couch and watched some TV together. I think we watched The Nanny until the end of the episode, then put the kids to bed.

That evening was unusual as Jeanette and I cuddled on the couch and watched more TV. I don't remember what we watched; it was just that I felt at home for the first time in a year. I had forgotten how soft and delicate her skin was and how beautiful she could be. Even with her being dressed in normal clothes that were more for comfort than looks, I didn't care. It was just nice to have her getting close to me again. I blushed a little when she kissed me, too, but that was the last thing I remember until she went to bed.

I know I had fallen asleep on the couch, even with my wife begging me to come to bed with her. I had determined to sleep next to her that night, but something stopped me. I did wonder up to the second floor and stood in the doorway as she slept, watching her torso rise and fall with every breath. I thought about how creepy it would seem if she woke up, so I moved from there and walked by Nicole's room. I remember looking toward the window and being drawn to it. I looked outside but saw nothing other than the normal sights.

Though the back yard was dimly lit by the light from the pole on the corner of the house. Otherwise, the whole area would be pitch black. I could hear Nicole sleeping soundly to my left, but I didn't wish to wake her. I turned just a bit and thought I saw a woman in a white gown standing in the yard and looking up at me. When I looked again, nothing was there, so I shrugged my shoulders and checked the locks on the doors again. The last thing I remember from that summer was going to bed that night, and I think sometime in July, it was the swimming class graduation. The kids did really well in showing that they could swim and what form they had. Brianna was new to swimming, but she passed the lessons regardless."

"So, what was the next thing you remember from that year?"

"I'm not saying right now. You know that I am done, so let me out of here, and I will come by tomorrow."

"I am afraid that will not be possible. If we are to gather more information, then we will see you at your apartment."

"How did you know that I live in...?"

"It is of no consequence to you. We know a lot about your life that you cannot understand. Not to say that we have been watching, but we have been investigating this matter long before contacting you."

This revelation visibly shook John, but he tried his hardest to keep his cool. He just stood from the table and said goodbye to the agent. The door to the room opened to allow him to leave, but no one seemed to open the door. At least, he could see no one on the other side of the door. He walked briskly to the lobby and then toward the door. As he did, he passed a man in a black suit with a black hat that had his back to John. He never saw the man's face, but the guy's skin seemed odd. Like really pale and clammy, as if he were a corpse that had been propped up and dressed in this suit. The sight creeped John out, so he felt it better to leave quickly.

After exiting the building and walking a short distance, John's stomach growled. He was once a man who had a large and somewhat imposing stature, but with everything that had happened, he was now skinny and frail looking. 2001 had started like any other year, but it seemed to be more rain than anything. May had brought rain like no other in the years before, and New York City seemed more dreary than usual. The only thing that had changed was the lowered crime rate, which gave the city more life with all the people coming out and enjoying the amenities available. Say what you want but everyone knew that Old Rudy led the city like no other.

John hurried to his apartment anyway to get out of the rain but felt as though he was being watched with every step. He couldn't see anyone watching him as he hunched further into his coat and walked faster. Upon entering the building, he checked the mail but found nothing but credit card offers and bills. Some he could pay, and some he thought about taking a credit card out to pay. Though he knew this would make things worse. He missed the days of being a high earner in society as a train engineer, but his current work seemed good, too. He worked for Central Park as a grounds manager and was paid fairly for his work. Though, it seemed that nothing would ever be as good since the 90s had come to an end.

He rode the elevator to the fifth floor, trudged his way to his door, and then entered the dark apartment. It wasn't the best place he could afford, but the rent was easily manageable for his income. So he lived slightly below his means, allowing him to travel when he wished. Working for the city gave great benefits that he could never have thought to be blessed with. He locked the door behind him while pulling everything from his pockets and hanging them by the door.

John had become used to living in the dark as much as possible, as his eyes had become sensitive to the light of the world. He only turned on the overhead kitchen light and left it at that. The rest of his apartment would remain in darkness until the sun rose from behind the clouds in the morning. He undressed and slipped into his pajamas, then settled in for the evening. The time was only 4:30 PM, but he knew that he would not have to leave the house again.

Some weeks before, he had been informed that the city selected him to undergo an investigation to which he thought was some police practice thing, but it seemed much more now. He had only agreed to the study in his boss's office before being visited at work by "agents" as they stated, and then escorted into their car. Since then, he had been instructed to go to a random and nondescript building three blocks from his apartment.

It was a nice break from his usual work, and he paid a lot of money that he had not been able to make since moving back to the city in '97. Though now he had no use for that kind of money other than to save it as much as he could.

3

"**M**r. Dorsett, are you alright?"

The artificial light of his apartment bothered his eyes even on this sunny day, but he could do nothing save for turning the lights off. He thought that would be rude to leave his guests in the dark. They had introduced themselves outside his door around seven in the morning and told him that three of them were to arrive, but at that moment, only one stood in his doorway. He could not say for certain, but John felt as though three were present even though he was not able to see them.

"I'll start in October of 93 if that suits you guys. I don't really remember anything that was important to your file before that.

So, the air had turned cold and crisp early in October, but I was not bothered since the fireplace was burning again. The house was nicely built to conduct the heat to other rooms, but there seemed to be limited pockets of cold air. I don't know how, but they were a fact of life to us. My kids would only complain if they stepped into a cold spot when leaving the shower or coming in when it was raining. Halloween was sure to arrive in three weeks, and I knew the children were becoming restless to be out for that holiday.

I don't think the school released them normally for such things, but Halloween fell on a Friday, and the school closed for half a day for it. It seemed nice that they would do such a thing, and I really welcomed my kids being home for a half day before rushing out to trick or treat. Work had taken on a life of its own as we had been given projects to fix the rails as quickly as we could before winter. It wasn't hard work, but tedious as we had to inspect the railway behind every train that would pass.

Everything had gone well, though, and it seemed to be busy work as the freight had begun to slow a bit before November. So, we all would board a platform and ride the rails for the inspection. I don't remember who had talked about it, but someone had described the area that I lived in as a spooky place. I laughed and replied, "No more creepy than any other dark place in these mountains".

I noticed that his eyes grew wide as he realized that I lived in that area, and I provided him with a broad description of where my home was located. Everyone fell silent at that moment, and I could not understand why. Apparently, they didn't wish to rag on the area but felt it important to mention it. I keenly surmised that they wouldn't have said anything if they had known that I lived there. So I spoke up after a moment of silence, "What is wrong with the area?"

They didn't say anything at first, but the asshole on the team bluntly put it, "That place isn't right, man. I've heard things from people who have lived there, and they all say the same thing. DON'T LIVE THERE!" That was all he said at first until I had begged for an explanation. I said that anyone who had the balls to tell me would get fifty bucks from my next paycheck.

"Hey man, fifty bucks is fifty bucks! You want to know, then listen up. You live in an area that seems to be haunted by something no one has seen. I don't know how to break it to you any other way, but come the end of October, you and your family are fucked."

He could see that I was irritated by his wording, but he obviously didn't care in the least.

"Something comes around in that area so late in the year; no one has ever been around long enough to know. There is a reason very few houses are there and the locals know to lock everything at night and not go out after dark. Some have seen a woman in a white gown and said she does things, but I never could hear any details. This is along with other shit that a guy in Fairmont would puke every time I asked him about it."

This struck me as odd as I had never known any of this before moving into the area. However, the memory of seeing the woman from the corner of my eye flooded back. I knew then that this shit could all be true, but what would I do with that information? So I did what I could to alert Jeanette. She shrugged it off and laughed about it as rednecks being rednecks, and that was it. Though I did feel a truth to it all, as I had felt and heard subtle things until that time.

Eventually, I also put it out of my mind, as I had not seen anything further until before Halloween. I think it was Wednesday, and I had taken the rest of the week off after we completed our inspection project. I focusedon fixing the house in the mornings and spending my after noons walking about the area. I looked for any indication of someone coming on my property but found nothing. The mention of that girl was not fresh in my mind but had now become a slight concern.

That evening, in particular, I would see Jeanette returning home with the kids late, so I went to The Beehive in Fairmont. I don't think I had been there long when I overheard two older guys at the other end of the bar talking about strange events in the area. I could tell they were reminiscing about the "good ole' days" as they spoke fondly of some of these stories they heard. What was odd was when I moved close to them and butted into the conversation.

"Evening fellas! You both mind if I ask some questions about the area?"

The both stared at me and then at each other before replying, "Sure! What do you want to know?"

I lit a cigarette after offering them one, then asked, "I moved to the area back in June, and since you both were talking about odd stories in the area, I thought you might know something about 766 Middletown Road".

Both of them turned pale as a ghost and began closing their tab.

They left the bar without another glance with the last guy looking at me with sadness and shaking his head before closing the door behind him.

"What the fuck?" I thought.

That was the first moment I knew something was up about the property we had purchased. At first, some guys at work were talking about it, and then two guys left the bar that I was in as if I were the devil incarnate. I couldn't make sense of why everyone would just be afraid of a woman with a white gown being seen. Surely, she is just an annoying haunting, and that is the extent of it. Though, I had never known anything of a haunting or the like. I thought about it for another couple of moments before putting it in the category of odd things that happen in this area, and that was it.

The only other indication that something was off was how the bartender looked at me as I continued to sip my whiskey and take another pull of my cig. He seemed disturbed and shocked at my stupidity or ignorance on the issue. I just went on about my time there at the bar, only to leave some hour later for home. By this time, I had purchased a brand new F-150 Lightning. I piled into the truck and got the heat going as quickly as possible. The sun had finally started going down by this time, and the air was nippy, to say the least.

I raced back home along the back roads from Fairmont to my home just to get off the highways and have a scenic route to enjoy the mountains. I don't know how it happened, but I pulled into my driveway to see the Sheriff sitting just beside the front door of my home."

John laughed slightly, with less of a laugh than a quick forcing of air from his lungs. All of this with a slight smile on his face. He took a sip from his coffee, followed by a drag from his cigarette again.

"I was convinced that my wife had had an accident on some back road, and the worst had come true. Though at the time, I wouldn't have laughed."

I pressed firmly on the gas pedal as the modified 390 blasted to the top of the driveway, only for me to pull in behind the officer. I put it in park with the emergency brake on, then leaped from the cab within seconds. I rushed to the officer who would sat in his patrol car. He rolled the window down as I approached.

"Is everything alright, officer?"

"Everything is fine for you, but not for us."

This shocked me slightly as I wondered what he was talking about.

"Get in the car, and I'll explain something to you, boy!"

So I entered his car in the back seat. I thought I had no choice but to comply in case something had gone awry and I was to blame for it. The sound of his voice was less about something horrible happening than extremely authoritative. I just remember that he moved the rear view mirror so that he could look into my eyes from where he sat.

"I have heard from the bar that you have been asking about strange goings on around these parts. Is that true?"

Again, I was dumbfounded as I sat there staring back at the man. How in the fuck did he know that I was asking a simple question, and who would have called him?

"I asked you a question, boy!"

"Yes, sir, I had been told about something odd going on around this area, but no one will tell me what it is. I have a family, officer, and I need to know anything I can to keep them safe."

"You mean you purchased this home from the realtor without asking anything about the area? Are you fucking dumb?"

"What kind of officer asks a question like that? With all due respect, how the hell would I want to know anything other than purchasing a house for my family? It seems so quiet around here, so I assumed that it was just a remote area."

The officer sighed and removed his hand, then placed it in the seat beside him.

"Let's go for a ride."

With those words, he shifted the car into drive and pulled away from the house and then down the driveway.

"What's your name, son?"

"My name is John Dorsett, sir. Am I in any kind of trouble?"

"Not really, but you have made things so goddamned inconvenient for me. I don't like paying people a visit about this kind of shit, so I will be frank with you. I know that you don't seem like a bad guy and more so that you're only concerned with caring for your family. I can relate to that, but you out-of-towners really fuck things up since no one told you the truth."

"What is the truth?"

The officer turned right onto a different road I had never been down before, then drove a short distance before pulling off onto an asphalt partition.

"West Virginia is steeped in odd events and occurrences. I know that much should be apparent to someone like yourself, Mr. Dorsett. Anyone who doesn't know as much will quickly find out. So here I am to inform you on matters I would rather forget. Most people know enough to keep quiet about living here and anything that goes on this far outside town."

"Some people have called us over the years to report odd sounds from the woods around their home. When we arrived to check it out, the caller went missing, and dispatch could only say that the line went dead. Most newcomers to the area don't know enough to stay in their homes after the sun goes down, such as now. I don't want to be an inch closer to your home at this point, and this little spot is just beyond the strange things that happen."

"We have never been able to investigate any of this shit to a satisfying conclusion, and I have been sheriff for a long time now. As soon as we get the call and rush to the area of the caller, nothing is ever found unless they are in their home at the time of calling. Most people see something so odd that they pull the cord to the door and are calling from their porch. So we had to implement a policy for dispatch to determine the area of the caller and then advise them to go back inside quickly before continuing their report."

"Most comply immediately, but some don't seem to understand. However, this was all years ago. Eventually, the calls from this area stopped coming in altogether, and we assumed that meant that the people who have lived here for a long time were the only ones left.

That or the newcomers either vanish before they can call or they are told by others, so they stay inside and don't go out to look."

The sheriff breathed another sigh, wiped his forehead, and hung his head as if to the memory of those lost.

"John...I'm so very tired of hearing of people going missing out here. My job is to protect the community and those in it, so forgive me if I feel I have failed the citizens here. I know that people go missing here to this day, but people have stopped reporting it."

The sheriff looked in the rearview mirror again and said, "Do you know what it's like to pledge my career to protect the public around here only to have them vanish before you can? It's fucking disheartening."

He paused again for a moment before pulling back out onto the road. This time, he was driving the speed limit back to my house. He said nothing until we arrived back at the front of my house, only to let me out of the car.

"Mr. Dorsett, I know I haven't said specifics, and I won't. I'm glad to have you in the area, but please heed this warning: Don't, under any circumstances, go out at night around here. Try to arrive home at a decent hour before nightfall and do not investigate anything. If you ever need help, then call me."

The sheriff handed me his card with his number on, then immediately motioned for me to enter my home. As I did, Jeanette arrived with the kids, only to see the sheriff enter his car again and leave. She looked puzzled, but I simply ran out to help her get the kids in quickly, shut the door, locking it behind me. My mind raced with the information as I set the kid's things down from school and worked to get them ready for bed.

It all made sense now: the locks on the back door only, the windows being nailed shut, all of this, and the odd happenings some months before. A slight tingle ran up my spine as I came to terms with this information. I knew that Eric suspected something was off with me, but I would not tell him any of this. Instead, I gathered them together and made it clear that they were not to leave the house after dark for any reason.

I then put them in their beds one by one as Jeanette was changing into her night clothes for bed. I had just hoped she would listen to my warnings as the kids had. However, I knew she would ask way too many questions. I simply slipped into the room to see her taking off her pants and exposing her beautiful body with nothing but a thong on. I know you guys don't want those details, but that memory stuck with me. It had been months since I had seen her naked, and I could not think of anything better to do at that moment than give into our lusts.

I say that to say this: after making love, I informed her of what had happened with the sheriff and why he had visited. She didn't think much of it and seemed to dismiss my words and even my presence. However, this time, I didn't grit my teeth and bear it.

"Why the fuck do you do that shit? Do you have a problem with me or our marriage?"

She said nothing else and just rolled over to go to sleep. I heard the click of the light and I could feel the anger and frustration building in my chest. I simply left the room and went downstairs to watch some TV. I had no reason to be up in the morning other than to make breakfast and help Eric get ready for school. I just remember being pissed that she was ignoring everything that I had said to her, but I couldn't understand why.

The rest of my nights were spent sleeping on the couch in the living room. Well... those were the nights that I would get some sleep. You see, something had begun to work in our home from then on. The kids seemed distant as well, and I became suspicious that Jeanette was telling them shit to drive them away from me. I would not have been surprised in the least if she had slapped divorce papers on the table one evening and told me that she was leaving and taking the kids back to Richmond. Though it didn't really happen like that.

So, that night, I sat up until 10:30PM watching TV. I think I had like three beers that night, but I am certain that what happened that night had nothing to do with simple drinking. I think it was around nine that I began feeling like I was being watched from behind. I sat with my back to the window that looked out onto the backyard and the same toward the doorway. I turned to look toward the doorway and could see nothing, but I felt a chill begin within the room. My instinct was to get a fire going in the fireplace to warm the rest of the home.

I worked to get the wood into the fireplace, then made a little house with the kindling around the logs. I threw some newspapers in there and lit them on fire. I sat on the couch again until around 9:45, only to realize that the room was still cold. I couldn't understand this as I was two feet from the fireplace that now held a raging fire.

I looked around again and decided to stand and stretch for a moment to warm my body. I also looked about the back door, but it was still locked. I poked my head into the hallway and looked about the area, but I could see nothing. I didn't want to wake anyone up by turning on more lights in the house, so I lit a lantern in the kitchen. The light glowed brightly enough to see what was around me.

No more than a second after lighting the lantern, I heard what sounded like a little pitter-patter of feet moving around in the dining room. I walked into that room and held the lantern out to see nothing out of place. No children were hiding in the dark or looking for a late-night glass of water or snack. I thought this was odd but turned to enter the kitchen again when I saw something rise from the corner just beside the back door. It looked like Nicole rising from behind that short wall and corner and walking slowly back toward the stairs at the front of the home.

I looked toward that area, but she had already moved behind the other wall beside the opening to the hallway from the dining room.

"Nicole?" I called out.

I hesitantly moved to the doorway and peeked into the dark hall-way. I couldn't see anything but held the lantern into the hallway to be sure. It became apparent that the basement door was standing open, and the new locks that we had put on it were hanging from their latches. We had to use chain locks since the doorframe had been too worn to put in standard locks. So I installed them to go from the door around the corner to the left of it and attached them to the locking slide on that wall.

It was odd but effective in sealing the door shut so the cold air from below wouldn't filter into the upper levels. I understood now why the living room had become so cold and refused to relent. So I went to the basement door and began to shut it until I saw something from the edge of my vision. I peered into the darkened space with the lantern stopping at the bottom step below me. I could see a pale figure standing there making no sound and looking down at its arms. I couldn't tell if it was a man or a woman, but I knew they were there. As I watched this person for a moment, their arms grew longer and longer. It was like a tree was growing its branches at increased speed, but with a person's arms.

This continued until the hands reached the floor then they looked up at me to reveal the fucking thing had no face! I jumped back and slammed the basement door shut, then latched the chains as fucking fast as I could. I had never witnessed anything like that before or since. I remember standing there in the dark with the lantern in my left hand and staring at the now-shut basement door. I don't know if I was waiting for this thing to come to the door and start beating on it to get into my house. Or if I was having a vivid dream, but the latter was proven wrong when I decided it was better to move back into the well-lit living room.

I blew out the lantern and set it on the floor beside the couch. I watched TV until 10:20 PM, but I was not going anywhere near that fucking doorway. Instead, I sat in the chair right in front of the TV and continued watching until I fell asleep. I don't know how long I was out before I awoke again to see that the fire had burned down but was still radiating a lot of heat into the room. At that moment, I turned the lights off and the TV, got onto the couch, and covered myself. My sleep was uninterrupted from that moment until Jeanette woke me to help with the kids the next morning."

John sat in his recliner smoking his cigarette, his hand shaking constantly as he brought the filter to his lips and inhaled.

"I apologize, but that shit still fucks with me to this day. I don't know why the hell the arms were growing, but I can never unsee that stuff. I know that I will have nightmares as I have before, but they will happen again tonight."

"Then you can understand why we must be quick about these interviews. We need the truth at any cost, but dragging this out only hurts yourself, John."

"That's the first time you have used my first name, and I find it really off-putting."

"Would you rather that we refer to you as Mr. Dorsett?"

"Frankly, I don't give a fuck. Just give me a moment to gather myself, and I'll continue from where I left off."

"While you're doing so, I wanted to ask about your children. Did they see anything like what you have described?"

"That is for later in my story."

"Very well, and do you remember animals acting strangely in the area? What about any cows, sheep, or dogs? What were their mannerisms?"

John laughed for a moment as he looked the agent in the eyes.

"What kind of fucking question is that? You guys on acid or something? I don't know what mannerism a damned cow or sheep would have. Yeah... I walked out of my house, and a sheep told me that the shit around that house was freaking him out and to knock it off. You guys are fucking weird as hell."

The "agent" seemed to sit back in his chair as if to be offended. He didn't say anything.

"Sorry if my bluntness was too harsh, but I didn't pay any attention to animals in the area except a couple of geese that started showing up the day after Halloween. That would have been the Saturday after the events that I just told you.

I guess I first noticed them that morning as I was up before anyone. I remember going to bed early and getting a lot of sleep. It's like peace fell upon my home that night, and nothing could have awoken me or my family. I was looking out of the kitchen window to the side yard and saw two Canadian geese staring back at me. I know what these types of geese normally do as they strut around the yard and eat stuff from the grass. These fuckers, however, just stood there and watched me while I watched them. They would show up early in the morning but always out of that window.

I thought I was losing my damn mind when I went to the window that faced into the same yard from the dining room, and they weren't there. I then walked back into the kitchen, and they were still staring at me. I hate Canadian geese anyway cause they are dickheads in every sense of the word, but yeah, they were just there. Even more odd was that they would never show up at any time other than early morning, from what I could tell, and would vanish when looking toward them from any other window. If you went outside, then it was like they would appear in the sky as if flying away.

I asked my wife if she had seen them, but she always stared at me then told me what she had to do that day and when she would be home. Though, at some point, she would have difficulty coming home at the right hour. She would call, and I would have to pick up the kids. I knew she was having an affair, but what would I say? I just didn't want to think about it and concentrated on caring for my children. I knew also that I would go the hell off and probably bash her head in with something. I don't know why, though. I had begun to become more angry and frustrated with my life.

I wanted to blame it on that house, but I couldn't tell if it was the house or if it was myself growing tired of being abused in such a way. I also determined that anything to be done about it would require evidence, but I had no time to collect such information. Instead, I focused on my children, as I have stated, and I tried not to think about the rest. Jeanette would come home late and say she was tired from work, kiss me, and go to bed. I wanted to go to the accusing phase, but I knew she would just deny it adamantly.

Anyway...The day I first saw the geese was different because we were all home the whole day. I played in the yard with Nicole, Eric, and Brianna while Jeanette made breakfast, lunch, and dinner from home. She would call from the back porch, and we would run inside to get something to eat while watching TV. Then, we would rush back out to play again. We loved football and baseball in the back yard, which mainly kept our attention. Though, I remember seeing

Jeanette in the dining room window talking on the phone. I never knew who she was calling so much, but she didn't look happy about it.

Either way, nothing would happen until that evening. It was just after the sun had drifted below the horizon, and only a shade of light glowed across the landscape. Brianna came running toward me from her room and said she could hear someone yelling for help from the outside. I looked her in the eyes and said, "Don't worry, sweetie, it's probably just someone playing pranks. No need to look. I'll check it out".

I just smiled as she continued to look concerned, then left her sight and moved back downstairs. I would fiddle with the doorknob on the back door, then wait a moment before telling her I could hear nothing. She didn't seem to believe me, but eventually, she just shrugged and began playing in her room again. It had become easy to keep the kids inside by this time as I had prepared them subtly to just know to come inside before nightfall. I don't really know how their classmates wouldn't have said anything about the strange shit happening in the area.

Given the looks I would get when I told people I lived in that area, I was sure no one would tell them anything. So, I kept my mouth shut and stayed prepared in case anyone would say something to them about it. Though that talk would only happen once, but I digress. The screaming for help continued sporadically that evening until even Jeanette was suspicious. I told her I had heard nothing and acted like it had never happened. I knew she didn't believe me, especially since I had mentioned what the sheriff had stated. Still, yet, what would I say? I just kept playing it down and paid attention to what I was doing in those moments.

The time passed until around 9 PM, and nothing had really happened. Jeanette removed herself from the living room and went to her bed after a few minutes, which left me alone in the living room. I could hear her up there playing with herself as quietly as she could, but her room was almost right above me. I could feel the insult that this was, but I said fuck it after a few moments. I just let it pass so I wouldn't do something crazy. I had to tell myself that she kept me at a distance and not the other way around. She just seemed withdrawn, and nothing could be done about it cause I couldn't get near her.

I did the only thing I could do and crept up the stairs and entered the bedroom. She seemed startled as I did and yelled at me in a whisper to get the fuck out. I smiled and told her I could hear everything she was doing so she just looked at me like ok...and?

4

I moved back to the living room after scaring my wife and being scolded for coming into the room at such a time. We had fought, and she tried to make me out to be the bad guy, so I just left while holding out the middle finger. She could be a royal bitch by herself if she wanted, and I would watch some TV and relax. I know I was sitting on the couch thinking about where everything went wrong, only to blame myself. Even though I knew it wasn't my fault as I had always been supportive and cared for the kids as a father should. I had tried to talk to her about her feelings and any issues she was having, but she would hide stuff like always.

Eventually, I just let her check out and stopped trying to deal with her. So when I would see shit like I did that night, I said nothing to her and just tried to deal with it. The isolation would grow further, and I would just shoulder more of this shit alone. I also kept it all from the kids as much as possible so they wouldn't worry or be scared. Regardless of any of this, I sat there watching TV until I heard a slight scratching noise from the hallway. I thought it was one of my kids going for a snack at night, so I just looked into the hallway. The horror came over me when I realized that it was coming from the other side of the back door.

I dared not open the door and simply moved back into the living room. I sat there in my pajamas with my furry bear slippers on and tried to ignore it. Then, the room grew colder and colder again. I already had a fire going and just relegated to something that would happen regardless. Without thinking about it and as though I had just become accustomed to strange shit in my house, I walked to check out the basement door. It was still sealed shut, and I could feel no cold air coming in from around the door jam. It was as though the cold was leeching away the home's heat slowly and would follow me around.

I knew this to be the case as I would move away from the area I was in to feel warmth all around me. Shortly after, I would feel the cold creeping up until I was surrounded. I could breathe and see my breath every time. I just moved back into the living room and stoked the fire some more. I would finish by putting another log on the fire and then sit on the couch again. A few moments passed, and I could hear the scratching again. I was becoming annoyed with this already and moved to the window that allowed me to see the back porch. I peered out to see a young girl scratching at the back door.

I whispered, "What the fuck?" then the girl stopped. She turned and looked back at me as I could still hear the scratching again. This made me jump back toward the couch, only to realize that my heart was racing again. She looked different this time as she was in great detail. She was about 16 in age and looked to be unbothered by anything around her. That is to say that she had a blank expression that didn't change at all. She was quite developed, which made it odd that she would have worn such a small nightgown.

I don't even know how the gown could have covered all of her, but it did. I kind of laughed to myself inside as the term "sexy ghost" entered my thoughts. To be clear, I was around 25, so it wasn't as creepy as it would have been to notice such things, but I wasn't enticed or aroused by the sight. Instead, I was more confused than anything. Most ghost stories were about young women in long, flowing dresses. Either way, I continued to listen as she scratched on the door. I didn't wish to have anything to do with this anymore as I had had enough fright for one night. I just felt this deep curiosity come over me and take control of my body. My mind fought valiantly to stop me from looking out the window again, but I could not stop my body from doing so.

This time, though, she was not there, but the scratching sounds continued. It was a light scratching that wasn't caused by much force against the door. Before I could think further, I saw something move from the left of my vision, so I turned my head. She was staring at me from outside so I could only see her face, but she was screaming. I could not hear a sound, but the bitch was screaming, and that face! That face is something I will never forget. Her eyes were wide and pitch black, as though she didn't have any eyes at all. Her mouth was open very wide but no sound came out. I knew she was trying because her vocal cords were tight within her neck.

That was all the details I could get before jumping back from the sight. The whole thing lasted about two seconds, and I was back on the couch staring at the window and door as though she would come through to get me. She didn't, however, and I just caught my breath. I also didn't understand how she was related to the thing in the basement, but I was sure it all stemmed from the same thing. These beings were horrifying in every sense of the word, but not blatantly so.

I had finally stopped breathing so hard as the shock that had taken me over left, and the sounds of the house around me came flooding back. I tried to watch TV, but that scratching continued, and then a moaning sound like someone being trapped under a heavy object, began to emanate from the window and the door. My heart started racing again, and I just prayed that this would all stop soon. My heart and mind had reached a breaking point when it all stopped and silence reclaimed the house again.

That moment only escalated things as I could hear the latches begin falling off the basement locks, which was followed by the creaking of the basement door slowly opening. My heart sank within my chest as my adrenaline spiked again. My whole body became numb with fear, and I just looked toward the doorway that led out to the hallway and watched. I could hear the sounds of wet, naked skin slapping against the wooden stairs in the basement. The slapping continued to the top of the stairs, then stopped for a moment.

The silence was broken again by this same wet slapping sound entering the hallway and working toward me. I knew this thing was coming for me, and I would not understand the scale of terror until it reached me. I rushed to the fireplace and grasped a stick then lit it on fire. This thing would have a hard time taking me without a fight. I remember just sitting there, waiting as it crawled slowly toward the doorway, with the slapping sound continuing. Eventually, it seemed as though the sounds had begun to come from everywhere around me.

I couldn't understand how this could be possible in the least, but I was too scared to truly consider it. My baser instincts had taken over now, and I waited for this fucking thing to come around the corner and toward me. I knew that I would begin waving the flame around as I shit my pajama pants from fear, but nothing ever came. The sounds just suddenly stopped as quickly as they had started. The sounds of my heavy breathing flooded back into my ears, along with the pounding of my heart in my chest.

I could now feel the sweat beading down my forehead and then down my cheek. I drew in a deep breath, then exhaled a FUCK! as I clutched my chest. This seemed to have a calming effect, and all the energy and fear flooded from me, which left me hungry. I lit the lantern left in the living room as quickly as I could, then poked it and my head out into the hallway again. I shit you not. That fucking basement door was closed and locked. I even checked the locks and latches to find that they were still in the position I had left earlier.

There was no trail of wetness on the boards that led from the basement to the doorway of the living room. I just backed into the living room again and sat with my back against the TV. I must have sat there for like two hours and waited for this shit to get me. Nothing happened, and I fell asleep sitting up with the lights and TV on and the lantern still on. Jeanette discovered me and asked what the hell I was doing. I grumbled something to her, then stood and walked off.

"Come back here, John! I'm not done talking to you."

"What the fuck do you care, Jeanette?"

"I like you better when you pretend to work late while you're visiting with other men."

John chuckled nervously as the agent stared at him.

"Mr. Dorsett, laughing about infidelity is disturbing. I don't think you realize the impact of affairs on a relationship."

John gave a puzzled look to the "agent".

"Why would you reply in that way? I'm starting to think that you guys are aliens or something."

John laughed at the idea, but the "agents" did not join him.

"Sorry, but you don't seem to understand the finalities of human mannerisms. Maybe you can ask the cows and sheep to help you with that."

Once again, John laughed, but he was the only one in the room to do so.

"I thought that was funny, but I'll stop being an asshole to you guys. I know being in law enforcement seems to suck away your ability to find things funny.

However, Jeanette and I had a real fight about my statement and how I could be so spiteful. As I had thought, she denied any of it and stated that she was late at work. She even picked up the phone and called her friend who worked in the same office with her. After hearing the woman's voice on the other end, I just put the phone back on the hangar. I didn't care anymore about proving her wrong or trying to stop it. I just wanted to end the fight for the kids and move on with my life.

At that moment, I did what I do best. I jumped in the truck and left the house to calm down. I drove out onto the country roads around the area until I reached the curviest road I could find. I drove up and down it until I felt better, then pulled off where the sheriff had taken me that night. I smoked a cigarette and allowed a few tears to run down my face for a moment.

I had forgotten about the man walking down the road that I had passed a couple of times and was surprised when I heard a knock on the passenger window. I quickly dried my eyes and sat up in the seat. I rolled the passenger window down with the hand crank and asked if he needed help. He looked at me, puzzled for a moment, and then said, "I don't need help, but I think you do".

He just smiled in a friendly manner, but it was off-putting somehow. I don't know what he was thinking, but he acted like everything was ok. I looked around the truck and could not see any indications of distress from my vehicle or any other.

"I don't understand."

"You were driving around really fast in that shiny new truck. Had to be that you were pissed about something."

The fucker was right, and I had no capacity to deny it.

"Yeah, just dealing with a lot of family shit right now. Sorry to be rude about it."

"Awww, that's no problem, son. I'm old enough to see pain in a man's eyes, even without knowing. Do ya' think you could give me a ride back into Fairmont?"

To this day, I will never understand why I agreed to drive this guy up to Fairmont, but I did it without hesitation. I didn't feel he was a bad guy or trying to harm me, so I unlocked the door and let him in.

"Name's Bill. Nice to meet you, son. I appreciate the ride. I don't have anyone to drive me anywhere, and I lost my license cause I like to drink too much. Never hurt anyone, but the sheriff is really persuasive in such things."

"Good to meet you, Bill."

I shook his hand with a strong grip to not seem like a wimp. After that, I put the truck in drive, pulled out of the little side area, and went back onto the road.

"If you don't mind me asking, what's going wrong with that family of yours?"

"It's my wife, Jeanette. She has been very distant in our marriage for over a year and now she is coming home late almost every night. I have to leave work early almost every day to bring the kids home. She just checked out and can't remember when."

"Yeah...she is weighing her options in life. How old is she?"

I told him she was 22 and we had three kids together.

"Y'all are too young to be having issues like this. Where does she work?"

I told him that she works for the administrative office for the county.

"Hmmm...she ever give a reason for you to jump to cheating in your mind?"

"Yeah, I can't get her to be with me anymore. Been about four months since we have but maybe more."

"That's as good a reason as any to become suspicious. You ever seen her with any other men?"

I just shook my head and then looked back to the road.

"It's a damn shame when a young family faces issues like this. You ain't abusive toward her, are you?"

I just gave him a stern look.

"Hmmm, I thought not. You ever see her going to work looking really pretty or anything like that?"

I shook my head again. I could see that we were near the city and I was ready to hear any conclusion the old man had to offer.

"I had a wife once. Caught her with another man in my bed. I did what any man would do. I just crept up on them and put a twelve gauge to his ass, and pulled the trigger twice. Wasn't a pump gun either. I could hear them both screaming in pain and I bashed their heads in so they would shut the hell up. I spent six years in prison for it, but I felt good about it. Hell, that was back in 1973. Been twenty years since I killed the whore, and I have slept soundly ever since. Even in prison, I slept really well."

I just looked at him in amazement at the matter-of-fact way that he said it all. He then pointed to a parking lot that I could drop him in. I pulled in there as quickly as I could, and then he opened the door and stepped out.

"Word to the wise, A man can never allow his woman to think she can betray like that. You just get hurt in the end. Do what is best for you and you alone."

He then smiled like the old bastard just gave me a cookie and told me a fucking nursery rhyme, then shut the truck door and walked off. Needless to say I was silent the whole ride back home. I don't know much about Bill, as I never saw him after that morning, but I still remember it like it was yesterday. The guy was just so chill about murdering his wife and her lover. I will admit, however, that some part of me agreed with the guy, but I know that prison isn't a good option.

When I pulled into the driveway, Jeanette was smoking a cigarette on the porch. She had been crying and waiting for me to come back. I just pulled up and sat in the truck for a few moments and stared at her. Turning the truck off brought me back to reality, and I stepped out and walked over to her.

"I am sorry, John. I didn't know you would think that I was cheating on you like that. I have been working late and don't know how else to prove it to you. I'm not unfaithful, and I can promise you that."

"Then why the distance and disgust toward me? We don't even sleep in the same bed anymore!"

She held her hand out as if to say stop, then hugged me.

"I just don't know how to tell you that I cannot be touched right now. Something happened when Brianna was born, and I couldn't understand how to say it. It's like a switch went off in my head, and I see you as someone who will harm me by making me have another child."

She put her head on my chest and sobbed until I could feel her tears soaking into the fabric.

"I don't want to bear another child again, John. I just want to enjoy the life that we have without this fear. I just don't know how to shake it off and move on. I still just remember how happy you were when Brianna was born, and I know you expect that again."

I held her head up and said, "No. We have enough kids, and I don't think we can feed anymore."

We both laughed.

"I guess I can see why you would think that I am cheating, but this needs to change. I promise to work on accepting you back around me again, but it will take time. Just be patient with me ok?"

Her tears streamed down her face as I kissed her and nodded.

"I don't think that she ever worked it out cause she is an ex now, but whatever."

"Continue, Mr. Dorsett"

Anyway, we had a normal day until the night came again and I had to stay on the couch again. This night was different, however, as the sheriff knocked on the door around 10 o'clock.

"Sorry to bother you, Mr. Dorsett. Did you meet a man named Bill this morning and give him a ride into town?"

A fear seemed to rise within my chest as I was worried that I had aided a criminal or something.

"I did. Why? Am I in trouble?"

The sheriff shook his head and then looked me dead in the eye.

"I'll be brief, but Bill came up missing this evening. Did he say anything about leaving town?"

"No, sir. He didn't say anything other than why he was in prison for six years."

"Ah! Sorry to bother you so late. If you see him again, tell him to get down to the sheriff's office immediately."

I nodded, and the sheriff told me to have a good night and left.

"Did the sheriff seem to be nervous?"

"I didn't think so. He just seemed concerned and tired. That was all."

Either way, nothing was ever said about that night or Bill again. I just assumed he went somewhere and never came back. As I said before, I never saw that man again and still have no idea what happened to him. That was all that happened on the Sunday after Halloween. Except...the dreams started around that time."

"Tell us about those dreams."

I don't remember them very well as it's been almost eight years. My mind had no use for them after that house. I just remember one dream, and I don't know if I want to say anything about it.

"It could be important for our..."

"Yeah! The fucking file again, right? Sheesh, I'll tell you."

John lit another cigarette and took a deep drag, followed by a long and dramatic exhale.

This dream started simple enough as I walked through the hall and up the stairs of that house. I didn't seem like myself, at least not my age. It seemed that this was all from my perspective as a child. I never lived in that house before 93, so I don't know. I could hear noises like a lot of voices talking and laughing. I climbed the stairs and went to the room that Jeanette slept in. The lights were on, but no one was home besides me. That is until I rounded the doorway and saw several men having their way with her. She seemed happy and was just allowing them to do whatever.

Every thrust that the two men who were on top of her made brought my child self closer to tears. I couldn't bear it until everyone stopped and looked at me. It was her and like five men. I could see blood all over her, and the men's eyes began falling out of their heads. I could hear Jeanette as though she was alive, but she was covered in blood and wasn't moving. The men's arms began growing until they reached out and grabbed me. I only remember waking up on the couch in a cold sweat. The morning sun was shining into the room.

Everyone was gone from the house, but I was home for my last day of vacation. I remember eating some cereal until my engineering supervisor called and talked to me about an accident on the rails. He told me to take the next day off, and they would pay me due to an accident that had to be investigated before we could work again. I thought this was odd because they would normally want all hands on deck to assist. He said it wasn't necessary, though, and repeated to take the next day off.

I put the phone back on the hook and finished my breakfast before heading into the basement to see why the cold kept creeping in. I looked all around that place and found nothing but a broken window. Luckily, I had sealant and some cardboard to close the window and seal it shut again. My mind pointed to that window as where this other figure had been able to enter my home, and I was confident that it wouldn't be able to get in now. I finished that work and went outside to make sure it was sealed. Nothing seemed to be able to get in now, so I just left to run some errands. I picked up extra groceries and some cigarettes, then went back home. I would have bought some more rolling papers, but I hadn't found any weed since moving there.

The rest of the evening until Jeanette returned from work was uneventful, and I could not justify any fear I had felt the days and nights before. I think my mind had begun to have trouble trying to fathom what I had witnessed prior to that evening. The kids were moving around the house after school as I fixed something for everyone to eat. I don't remember what I had made, but it went well with the kids and Jeanette. While everyone ate and was content to do so, I went back out to the truck to grab the cigarettes that I had purchased, then lit them up as I walked around to the back of the house.

I wanted to ensure the window was still sealed after a few hours. I pushed the window and bit and pushed against the cardboard that had been taped over it as well. Nothing seemed to move in the slightest, so I considered my work completed at that moment. I looked up and could still see my family enjoying their food and time together as I rounded the corner of the house and then went back in the front door. No other windows seemed broken or missing on that side of the house either. Perhaps the other thing that grew its arms longer was a weird guy, and it was an optical illusion. Maybe he was entering the home through that broken window as he seemed slender enough to do so.

I couldn't be sure until the night fell over our home again. However, I decided to sit and eat with my kids and wife. That moment really spelled a turning point in my life, as it seemed that we were all finally coming back together. However, I wouldn't be able to relax until I could see that these events wouldn't terrorize me any further. I thought that it was really peculiar that they only happened to me and no one else. That is to say, besides the night, Brianna could hear the screaming for help from outside our home.

Oddly enough, the other kids still had not told them about the area that we lived in, nor did my wife seem to hear about that either. Instead, I just sat there enjoying her beautiful black eyes and chocolate skin as she ate her dinner and laughed with the rest of the family. She was different that evening for some reason that I could not know. I even remember asking her about it, but she would say nothing. I also could not say why she decided to get with some boring white guy and have three kids, but here we were, attempting to work it all out as a family.

Though I know it to be true, I cannot come to grips with the fact that that house took them from me, and I could not stop it. Every day seemed to push us further apart, and I never saw it coming. Sure, Jeanette had been removed from me since Brianna was born, but the house definitely added to it. I watched as that light I remembered from the day that we were married and shared many passionate nights together. That passion continued until after Brianna, but it seemed to show itself the month after she was brought home from the hospital.

The night ended with the kids going to bed and Jeanette spending time with me on the couch until she went to bed around 9 PM. I remember this as a Thursday night, but the girl never showed up, and no odd occurrences happened in the night. I walked Jeanette to the bedroom, kissed her good night, and then slept on the couch as usual. I remember waking to use the bathroom just off the living room, then went back to sleep, but nothing was out of the ordinary until the morning.

The door to the basement was standing wide open again without any reason. Jeanette was already at work that Friday, and the kids were at school as well. I remember calling her from the house phone and asking about the basement door, but she couldn't explain how the door was opened. She only would say that the kids had gone nowhere near the basement the whole time. I took her word, went outside, and hopped in the truck. It wasn't long before I returned to Fairmont and headed to the gun store.

After all this time, I don't remember the store's name as I was trying to get it as quickly as possible to go home and investigate the basement again. I decided to purchase a nice twelve gauge from the store owner. He had offered me an array of handguns, but I didn't wish to invest in that at the time. I remember going home and loading the gun as I went into the basement. I looked about the area in detail until I had come across that window again. Everything seemed normal, and nothing seemed to show, and entry for anyone to enter the house.

After that, I decided to make up the slides and chains for the locks on the basement door. No damage had been done to either of the components on these locks. I also didn't see anything indicating that someone had entered the house through the doors or windows. So I just stood in the hallway outside the basement and scratched my head. After that intensive investigation, I decided to move outside and have a smoke. I considered every point of entry, and nothing could explain it. Moreover, Jeanette swore that the basement was closed and sealed before leaving for work. I cannot explain that by house degradation or any other signs.

Now I am sitting here telling you that I still don't know how all these things got into the home."

"That is alright, Mr. Dorsett. We don't need an explanation, just the story. Please continue."

"Nothing of note happened until a few days before Thanksgiving. I think it was that Sunday before that everything went to shit quickly. I don't know if it was the freak from the basement or the girl outside, but something ripped the back door open and broke the locks in the process, but it didn't damage the door or the frame itself. I found this odd as it seemed that something had just broken the locks themselves and then pushed the door open.

It happened around 7 o'clock as we were all preparing for bed. Jeanette had taken to kissing me goodnight after putting the kids to bed and promising me that things would get better for all of us. I took that to heart as she looked like she wanted to be in love again. But as we kissed, the loud slam occurred with the back door, and I grabbed the shotgun and looked all around the house. I then checked the door and locks, shut everything up, and forced a chair under the doorknob to keep it shut.

For added security, I placed a long center block under the feet of the chair that were in the air. I felt this was the only way to ensure that someone or something could not get into the house. Jeanette and the kids were so shaken that they didn't sleep at first. I believe I put Brianna to bed around 9 PM that night, and she was finally off to sleep. This was a relief as the kids had to be ready for us to go to breakfast with my sister the next morning. My sister had come into town that Sunday evening and got a hotel room in Fairmont. I was sure we would have fun this week as everyone was off work and the kids school was closed.

Even to day, I still don't understand why the bulk of the happenings occurred when we were all at home vs. when we were gone for the day. Work had been going smoothly at this time, and I was happy with what I was doing and the money I was making. My marriage seemed to be looking up at that moment as I continued giving my wife the space she needed to get over everything. I didn't understand it, and in some ways, I didn't believe her, but that wasn't what mattered.

The rest of the night consisted of high winds that whistled past the windows and screams from the back door. I listened for anyone to stir from bed upstairs, but I didn't hear anything. The screams were barely audible, but I could hear them every so often. I kept the lamp near along with the shotgun in case anyone decided to risk the home. I can't tell you what I was thinking, as everything that happened seemed otherworldly, but it made me feel better to know that I could bury it with one blast of lead."

"Mr. Dorsett, this is all so fascinating, but when did everything happen more intensely?"

"I am getting to that part if you could give me time. Since it is nighttime already, why don't we continue this tomorrow?"

"We can agree to that if it will help you get to the point."

"Look...agent...I don't give a flying fuck how long it takes me. Don't rush my account, or I will refuse to work with you again. I know your threats, and I doubt they can come true. Just come back tomorrow, and my story will be where you need it to be."

The agents seemed visibly annoyed with John, but he showed them out.

"Mr. Dorsett, I expect to hear what I need to close the file tomorrow. We only have a limited time here. Well, with you, anyway."

"That will be agreeable. Just be careful with your horror show appearance around the city."

"Worry not, Mr. Dorsett. Our comings and goings are never known to anyone but us."

With that, the "agents" left John standing in his doorway. He had no more than looked to see what was making a sound to his right when he turned his head back and expected to see the men waiting for the elevator again, but they had vanished.

5

The next day came quicker than John had ever known. He awoke and stumbled into the kitchen as the coffee pot started brewing. The time was around 6 AM as John sat down at the table with his coffee and cereal. He just looked out of the window to the city and thought about his family. Surely, he would be able to find Jeanette and the kids again, but where would he start? Perhaps the "agents" would allow him to have that information. It would be a long shot to get any cooperation from them since they were more interested in the story than him.

They also never indicated that they cared a bit about his family or anything that had happened to them. John was starting to assemble the puzzle, and everything seemed to point to these men as being from another place. He didn't wish to say that they were deformed or in any way paranormal. He just knew that they were odd-looking. The lips were too thin, and the facial features appeared to be placed on the face in a grid rather than forming the person's identity. He couldn't be sure, but this was the assumption. Just as he had always done, John pushed these thoughts to the back of his mind and tried to consider something else.

That is when a knock came at the door, which startled the lonely man. He rose and answered the door only to find a package had been dropped for him. This was odd as it was too early for a delivery. He opened the package to find a listening device that seemed like a small speaker. The instructions told him to put it up to his ear and say, "John Here". He did as he was told, then an odd digital voice could be heard.

"Mr. Dorsett, you are being called to leave your home today. Come to the address on the back of the paper."

With that, the speaker cut out and then stopped. He threw it on the counter and began preparing for his commute. He knew the address as being near the local police precinct, though it seemed to be beside it rather than in the same building. At least, that is what MapQuest indicated to him. He then slid into a pair of jeans, a shirt, and a raincoat for the damp air.

The walk was not taxing or even difficult, but the weight of recounting his decisions gave him a heavy disposition as he trudged the way to the address. His fist held firm to the crumpled piece of paper that was his guide on this journey into hell. The further he went on, the more it seemed he had slipped between the fabric of this world and into another. This was a man who was oppressed not only by the weight of his decisions but also by the inability to be noticed in this time of strife. The air seemed to be light but cold, and the surfaces around the city were coated in a lining of water.

He sipped the coffee that he had packed for his walk and raised a cigarette to his lips every few steps. The only thing for John Dorsett to consider was the actions that he would now take in light of the revelations that his mind would not process but his soul held to firmly. Anyone could see his mind raced with these inevitable truths as he raced to some form of reckoning. Would it be that these agents would be forgiving of the hurried demands that they would make?

Just as he had begun to file his thoughts into an order that could be easily processed, he was already standing beneath the tower of foreboding that was his destination. All journeys had to face their inevitable end, and this minor odyssey would be seen to whatever end came. The building was not a large structure by any means, but the weight of his psyche had enhanced this place as a folly to be made. He forced his hand outward to latch onto the door handle in front of him as he could see a reflection that was not pleasing.

John had become more haggard with each passing moment of these interviews and could not reconcile with the judgements he had passed. It seemed that these weights brought about changes to his age and intellect. He was passable to societal standards but not to his own reflection. It would seem that he was the homeless wanderer that he had come to know himself since leaving West Virginia. He had been forgotten to a time that he could not accept rationally as it seemed too unreal.

The door swung open, and he entered with apprehension toward meeting another of these agents for yet another conversation on a time long lost. Yet everyone would say nothing and instead, stand as a stoic reminder of where to go and when to face his journey's end. Once again, he would sit in another interrogation room as he had before.

"Mr Dorsett, so good of you to join us. We will pick up with your story at the point we hope."

"As I had stated before, the bulk of the haunting, if you could call it that, came around Thanksgiving. I should've noticed the changes from this situation to my children as they had all become removed from Jeanette and myself. I knew that they were seeing things that we could not understand. I felt there was a hesitance to speak to us about things such as paranormal happenings, but I longed to fix that. Every time that I suggested talking about it, they would say nothing, and I didn't know how to handle that.

Eventually, you get to the point that your children resent you and your ability to invade their lives. So I gave them the space I thought they needed, but I don't think it worked. Last night, I thought about the things I did not wish to remember and think I can finally present them to you coherently. As a warning, however, I am not to be held responsible for what happened.

The week of Thanksgiving was odd for several reasons, but the main would be that I could not understand what actually happened vs. the dreams that I would have. Sometimes, I was convinced that I had seen my dreams within reality, and my reality had bled into my dreams. The Monday of that week came with a dream that horrified me. My guess was that I had this dream around 1 AM when I thought back on it. I was lying on the couch and could see myself lying there as if floating above my body. I could hear that same sound of wet flesh smacking against the ground that I had heard some months before. However, it was more pervasive and off-putting because it came from all around me.

The closer the sound became, the more it seemed to emanate from the walls themselves until every contact with the ground reverberated through my chest like a bass drum. I could not stop it as I could not convince my mind to wake up my body. The sound grew louder and louder until it was everything around me. Then, I saw arms extend beyond and into the limits of my vision. I saw them as pale and thin, as though the very veins within were hidden only by glass. They reached out as the figure that controlled them stepped into view.

It was that bastard from the basement come to attack me in my sleep. The arms reached my shoulders and began to lift and peel my body from the couch in a smooth and singular motion. I could feel the fear as though I were within my body again. This pushed me to wake up, only to see that nothing was there. I could only see the window before me and, to my left, the fire that still burned. I could no longer hear the sounds of the slapping flesh upon the ground, and it caused my mind issues as everything had been so real. I didn't know what to do except to calm myself by checking the basement door and windows. Everything was still locked.

I couldn't stop standing in the hall and looking in all directions while waiting for some abomination to enter the room and take me into the darkness. I fought the urge to run and stood like a statue, listening for more sounds to be made. After a few moments, I entered the living room and took my place on the couch again. My time had come to an end to be scared, but my heart still pounded lightly in my chest. I don't remember how long it took to fall asleep, but something seemed different when I awoke.

I could feel the house around me calling out to me. It was as though I was being tempted into falling for a trap by the home itself. I don't consider myself to hear voices, which was not like that. It was more like a feeling like I had become one with the home and whatever infested it. My family seemed normal somehow as it seemed to tire of toying with anyone else but me. I don't know what happened to that girl this week, but it seemed to be more of a creature that would stalk me now.

At this point, I had become phobic of entering the basement and trying to repair any more of the house. I relegated myself to the lower levels or the yard outside in the coming days. Thanksgiving seemed to bring the worst of it as tension had built in our connections as a family. Jeanette was against the kids and then against me. She had become worried about having any contact or connection as I seemed to be the one left in the cold. I had never seen a five-year-old girl like Brianna retreat to her room like a moody teenager. I tried desperately to bring peace to the house, but it didn't help. More often than not, I found myself alone.

Our actual meal was like any other, but my sister had been called back to Richmond with her husband falling ill. We all sat there in silence and anticipated the conversation that would come next. Jeanette continued with small talk to try to involve everyone in the meal, but it wasn't working. I would mirror her actions and nudge the kids to say more, but that didn't work well. A few seconds into our third attempt at conversation, it turned into a fright fest when the table was lifted from the middle of the room and slammed to the ground. A scream that was ear-piercing and terrifying filled the whole house. It sounded like a young child in agony and sobbing because she lost her parents.

I could feel both fear and sadness for the entity that made this scream while the rest of my family would lay on the floor until it was over. This was followed by the stove lighting itself and flames shooting three feet into the air. Then, everyone scrambled to the kitchen to put out the flames, but they continued. I yelled to Jeanette to bring the extinguisher as she stood in amazement and did nothing. Eventually, Eric would bring me the fire extinguisher for me to fail in putting the fire out. I yelled to stop in a tortured voice because I had become exhausted from all the torment and lost sleep.

The fire stopped only for the basement to fling open and begin slamming against the wall beside it. I couldn't do anything but rush into the hallway and attempt to close it.

I could see it, though. I knew this long armed thing was standing at the bottom of the basement stairs, watching us like a peeping tom. I was horrified that it had locked with my eyes and began phasing in and out of existence. Every time it would phase out, it became blurry like a photo. When it would reappear, it was a little closer every time."

Mr. Dorsettt now smoked just a little harder as he had gone through two cigarettes just recounting this event.

"I don't know if it was real, but it seemed so. Eventually, it appeared so close that I could see nothing by eyes and the flesh around them. The face was dead, with squinted eyes and no mouth. It was just skin covering what should have been a mouth. It screamed so loud that I yelled and jumped back against the wall. I couldn't feel anything pushing me backward against the wall, but the fear made me do that.

Try as we could, it took what felt like an hour to shut the door and put the chains back into their latches. My mind was flooded with the image of that being everywhere I looked. Every form of darkness harbored that character no matter what portion of the house that it was in. I couldn't stop the visions, no matter how much or hard I rubbed my eyes.

This creature was horrid as its arms continued to grow until it gave a wide and sinister smile that seemed to reach across its face as though the flesh of its mouth had ripped open. It was too much until I fell over a vent that stuck out of the wall slightly in the bottom molding. I felt the wooden floors slap me in the face as I bit down hard on my tongue. The visions seemed to stop for a moment until I rubbed my face and began to lift myself.

The being was in front of me as I continued rising from the ground. I was startled enough to go from being prone to being hunched against the front door and waiting for the creature to approach. But as I opened my eyes, nothing stood in front of me. I just don't know how to understand this in my mind, but it was more real than a simple hallucination. There were no words that could stop the terror from subsiding as I sat, forcing myself against the door and screaming out. Jeanette pulled me to my feet and kept asking what was wrong, but I couldn't find the words to tell her. I was just there pointing toward where the creature stood and yelling.

Our children retreated into the dining room and began hiding from anything around them. I knew that no one but myself could see what I had witnessed and now wondered what it was that I had seen or when it could come for them. This was the most horrifying thing in their minds. A few minutes passed after this incident, and I found myself with a cigarette just burning itself to the filter with the ash still sitting on its end. I sat on the porch with my feet on the lower step, just thinking about what I had seen.

Jeanette had begun to come closer as a loud crash occurred inside the home. She rushed inside to see what had happened, leaving me alone just staring at the ground and mumbling. I could tell that something major had happened and was continuing as she had begun to yell for my assistance. Just then, I was compelled to look up from where I stared, only to see the girl in the nightgown that was much too short. She just stared at me from the edge of the woods with a sinister grin.

I was forced to stand without losing eye contact and entering the house. I turned away from her as I shut the door only to see Jeanette fly from the dining room and landing on her butt, then sliding to a stop. When I looked to my left, I could see Nicole being pulled toward the upper corner of the room. My mind snapped into action as I rushed into the room and began pulling her back. I could feel Eric and Brianna pulling against my legs to help as they could.

I finally yelled out for the entity to let go of my daughter, and then she fell into my arms after such a forceful command. I held her in my arms as she sobbed uncontrollably just under where she was lifted. Jeanette called out for the kids as she reentered the room again. They rushed to her and huddled against her legs as I looked to see a face that I had never seen her make. She seemed broken and exhausted, which led me to believe that this had happened before when I was at work or something to that effect. I was sure of it now.

I took Nicole in my arms, lifted her up, and rushed everyone out of the home and into the truck. Jeanette hopped in the back of the truck and yelled for me to go. I struggled to put the key in the ignition and turn it as I heard Jeanette scream in terror. The switch finally clicked and gave way to turn the engine over and start the truck. There was a roar as the engine came to life and began revving until I dropped the shifter into drive. It didn't take long to peel down the driveway and out onto the road.

"I don't know how long I drove until we were back in town. I just remember that that moment was a continuous montage of stress and yelling while dashed with the sobs of my kids beside me. I eventually pulled over on the side of the road and jumped out to be with Jeanette."

John stopped for a moment and rubbed his forehead as sweat continued to dribble down onto his cheeks. The cigarette in his hand had extinguished itself.

"Jeanette described to me that she could see a girl phasing through the window and falling onto her head. She said that the girl's neck snapped in the most crunchy and audible sound she had ever heard. Then a scream emanated from the home that she described as being tortured."

"The girl fell from the second-floor window and broke her neck?"

"Yes, damnit! Sorry...I'm still startled by the image to this day."

"Continue, Mr. Dorsett."

I remember holding my wife in my arms as she sat in the back of the truck and sobbed. I could feel her tears on my skin and feel the pain of her heart at the terror of seeing and hearing the haunting herself. She confessed right there that she had been hiding the terror of what had happened to our children and herself. There was a disconnect to her voice, as if she didn't believe that it had even happened to her at all. This one event put us all on the same page in seeing things during this haunting.

We would spend the rest of the day out until night had fallen. Jeanette and I scraped enough money together to book a hotel for all of us for one night. I knew that everyone had become exhausted over the terror that we felt. Though, until now, I only knew of the struggles I had faced at the hands of these entities. My mind raced with possibilities, but nothing ever helps in those situations.

"You just never know what to do or say in those moments. But sometimes it's best just to hear the victim out and remember that you have seen just as bad, if not worse."

"Mr. Dorsett, do you know what happened at the house while you were gone?"

"I don't, as we had no way to record the incidents. I also didn't have any neighbors who would have checked on the house or were close enough to see anything. Where we lived, we were on our own."

"Interesting. Nothing further about that night?"

"Nothing to report. Though the next night seemed different."

John could tell that the agents were hard to read under normal conditions but now he seemed excited by something that he had just relayed to them. The agent who interviewed him seemed compelled to stand and walk robotically out of the room. Then, the door was shut to seal John into the room. He just sat and stared into the distance as he continued to smoke. His motions were more akin to an automaton rather than a living human. Habits had now taken over in the absence of higher thought and reason. However, John had come to know that the terror of those years in that house still lingered within his mind. Shortly, the agent returned and took his seat again.

"Mr. Dorsett, were there any other happenings in the town around you?"

"None that I could see, why?"

The agent ignore his question.

"Continue"

"What can I say? The next night was the same as Thanksgiving

Day. The only thing that happened after that for about a week was the dreams. I cannot remember much of the dreams other than waking up many times throughout the night. My work had begun to notice my fatigue until the head engineer called me into his office. He sat quietly for a moment and just stared at me from across his desk. I could hear the crinkling of his leather chair as he rocked back and forth.

"John, we are all worried about you. You are a great employee and have transferred here in good faith. I have no reason to second-guess your decisions and skill. What I cannot understand is why you have been so tired on the job. Mark and Elias have found you asleep at the engineer's station three times this week. Is something going on at home that we need to know about?"

I cleared my throat and stared at his desk for what felt like an eternity. I didn't know how to tell him that my house and its surrounding land had been haunted. So, I did what I had done before to see what reaction I would get.

"I live at 766 Middletown Road on the hill. What do you think?"

He stopped everything he was doing and told me to wait as he left the office. I could hear him go to the next office and begin talking with his boss. I could not make out what they were saying, but it seemed odd.

"I apologize, John. I didn't know that no one had told you about that area. I can understand why you are so tired. My boss also understands this as well. So, we are going to lay you off temporarily. Just for a couple of weeks to a month. This isn't a punishment, but I cannot have you falling asleep at your post. A lot of people could die if I continue to let you work in this condition. I know what you're going to say, and yes, you will get paid for this time out."

"Will that help you out?"

I just nodded as I continued to sit in my stupor. I really wasn't sure what was really and not real by this point. The only thing I did know was what my senses could tell me, which wasn't much at this point. I was grateful and fortunate to have such a great boss and workplace, but I didn't like being put out of work.

"Is there a possibility that you can move out of your home and to a different area?"

I just shrugged my shoulders and stared at his desk. He could tell that I could not process anything at that moment and called a work buddy over to take me home. After that, I blacked out.

The next thing I remember is coming to the guy's truck and being asked to get out of the truck. I hadn't even realized I was in my driveway outside my house. He asked me if I would be alright alone until my wife could make it home, and I just nodded and then slinked out of the truck and to the front door. I knew that he had driven away from the house and left, but I dared not turn around. The sleep that I had been pushing away came rushing back as I opened the door and fell into the house.

I don't remember what happened next, but the dreams had taken over. The only feeling I could understand was that of being pulled by my feet down the hallway and what seemed like down the basement's stairs. I had no energy to stop this being or even call for help. I couldn't tell if this was happening or if I had been dreaming it all. After all, I could not see what was dragging me along. I was along for the ride, and that was the extent of it. I tried to feel fear or scream, but I couldn't muster the strength to do so. Instead, I was compliant with any demands the being would make.

Abruptly, the dragging sensation stopped, and my feet were dropped to the ground of the basement. My eyes rolled around in my head for a moment as I could see a pale and slender entity slowly walking toward me. The sound with each step was that horrible, wet slapping sound. The only image that I had as I lost consciousness was its face breaking open to reveal a void that was in the shape of a smile. Once I witnessed this, my mind dragged me into the dream world.

I felt comfort and peace somehow as within my dream, Jeanette was holding me after a night of raucous sex. She was soft and supportive, along with whispering in my ear that it was all going to be okay. I could feel my mind and soul letting go of the pain and sadness that I felt toward her. I was becoming desensitized to the idea of dying right then and there. I had finally found the love from my wife that I had craved for over a year. Yet something told me that real life was not this way.

I don't remember much more than that about the dream or whatever it was. I just know that I cannot quantify it in my mind as real or not.

I could now see the events of my childhood flooding through my mind as Jeanette began to fade. The perversion of my formative years had begun as I could see my parents only scolding me into submission. The beatings that I know I did not sustain at the hands of my actual parents. The sinister faces of my children laughing from the edge of my darkened vision. They taunted me as they danced around and began eating pieces of each other's flesh. I fought as hard as I could, but I caved to the exhaustion. No one was coming to my aid, and I would soon become a shell being controlled by this entity.

At least, this is what I thought. I awoke to the sounds of Jeanette calling my name, along with the feeling of her trying to rouse me. I felt the fear within her as though she was projecting it into me, and I knew she was breaking all the same. This was the point that I knew we would never be ok again. Our family was gone at that point, as I had failed to protect my own children and wife. They were good to me, but I could not muster the strength to fight back. I suspect that this thing had been violating our minds and souls, forcing us into anger and fighting.

The peace within that home was over, and I could not understand how it had gotten to this point so quickly. I felt alone and lost, without any strength to push away these troubles and leave this home. We had no money saved, but I was sure to call the realtor to sell the home once more. The last portion of this memory was being helped to my feet and guided up the stairs. I was then placed against the wall as Jeanette was pushed to the ground and held down. The entity was not done with us, and I could no longer stand it.

I could do nothing but watch as she was being slapped and thrown against the walls of the hallway."

John began sobbing as he spoke.

"She called out for my help, and I remember it all. I could do nothing but sit there and watch this thing throw her around like a toy. I could see no one doing it either, and no contact was being made between her or anyone else to explain the floating. She began crying this instant as I did, which told me that our hearts were breaking. I made weak attempts to banish this being as I faintly called out for it all to stop.

Jeanette was then slammed into the ground, followed by intense screaming as she pissed herself from fear, followed by blood flowing down her legs. That was the moment that the sheriff and priest entered the home and began carrying her out. I was then gathered and removed from the home as I called for her to return to me. We..."

"I am sorry, but I cannot continue with this. I just can't."

John Dorsett crumpled to the table while only holding his head up with his hands. He cried tears that began in a deep and tortured part of his mind. The pain had now welled up and into his heart, which left him broken once again. The images of that evening flooded his mind and took him over. He no longer cared who could see him coming apart as he lashed out and threw his coffee cup across the room. The agent had vanished from the room without explanation as John proceeded to break down.

He raged about the room for a few moments, then ended by collapsing into the floor in the far corner of the room. He held his head in his hand. There was only the feeling of failure and depression that had begun flooding into his head. The pain only grew as he remembered the way that Jeanette would stare at him as she was being taken into an ambulance.

These were the moments that had come to signify the degradation of his family at the hands of these beings. The torment only grew from there until he remembers feeling numbness and slumping over. The next moment would see him rising from his bed in his apartment without any memory of arriving there.

6

The next three days were filled with sadness that seemed to come from John's soul as he would spend this time in bed. He did not eat, nor did he drink. He was now a broken man who was forced to relive the torment of losing what he had held dear. The shell of who he had been and who he would be in the future unless he could heal his mind. The images from his mind of seeing where the blood had soaked into the wood flooring from his wife filled his mind. The feeling of never being able to recover from something like that was ever present within his mind.

How could a man be utterly destroyed as the protector of his home and family without losing his sanity? Nothing could point to healing being possible from such an event, along with his kids being taken from him in court. The self-hatred and deep grief served to help Jeanette take the kids from him. Prior to that day, there was a resentment from childbirth, but after, there was a sense that she had been violated, and he simply watched. She seemed to never forgive him as the man he was in life.

He spent years recovering from this, which saw heroin and crack use on the streets of the city. He had fallen only to hit rock bottom;

worse now was that he would do it alone. Jeanette had vanished along with his kids and been a ghost in the life he longed for.

It was only after many cold and sleepless nights, along with being attacked several times that he learned to count what few days he may have left. Loneliness would be his teacher as he would pull himself from this dark place some three years later. This was the man who had been broken by the paranormal and an entity that seemed demonic in every way. No friends were waiting to assist in his recovery, nor any love interest to get him clean. He would be faced with his own mortality upon waking to find the young guy next to him, lifeless and pale-faced.

The drugs had taken the young man, and John feared that he would be next. He knew that he was broken, but would he really wish to be dead from these events? The only option left was to seek out the parish within the city and attempt to cleanse his body of the drugs. The only help he would receive would be from the nuns, who would care for his wounds and fatigue from the withdrawals. There was still no comfort that was familiar to him then, and when he came out of it, he had lost most of his body mass. A man who was once burly and capable now seemed ruined and frail from the chemicals he had shoved into his veins. The world seemed darker but somehow better now that he had been able to reclaim himself from the cusp of oblivion.

These were the memories that filled his mind throughout this time that he lay in bed and writhed in mental anguish. The only reprieve he would have was the phone call he would receive. It was an odd call but a memorable one that marked the end of his self-loathing. He freed himself from bed and forced himself to get the phone call. It was as though some other force of good had lifted him from his failure and brought him to salvation.

The other end of the call seemed grainy, but he could make out a woman's voice saying his name.

"Hello? Can I help you?"

"I am sorry for everything that I put you through. I know that you have been thinking about me and what was. Don't blame yourself, John."

Once the realization had set into his mind that this was the sound that he had been waiting to hear for the last three years, he snapped to reality. A renewed vigor overcame him as he knew he was still living for a better reason. Jeanette had called and brought herself back into focus within his life. However, before he could say anything, the phone went dead, and now only the dial tone could continue after the sound of her voice faded.

He was alone again and had nothing to show for it other than the peace her words had brought to his heart. He had finally been able to reconcile that he could have done nothing to assist his family, and they could have done nothing for him either. The blame had ended, which left an empty man who had nothing to lose in the end. John was convinced that the agents had contacted her and coerced her into calling him.

Something within his mind seemed to break as he could feel his thoughts flowing freely without the constraints of laws and rules. Everything seemed possible at this moment.

He moved with a speed and grace that John Dorsett had never possessed before as he moved to his closet and removed a box. He could feel the weight within that attempted to drag the box from his hands. He resisted this while placing the box on the end of his bed. One motion would see him removing the box lid and taking out a Smith & Wesson 45 and an additional magazine.

He dressed himself without thinking about any step to get to that point. John then slid the low-profile holster onto the belt and tucked it into the right side of his pants. With one motion of his hand, he placed the gun into the holster, and then began slipping on his coat and shoes. He was not stupid enough to take on a whole agency, but insurance was needed in this fight.

John then left the apartment and ensured the door was secure. He was a different man than the one he had been weeks before. These entities had changed him, and the memories of that place had brought him to his knees. He moved to the street and then traveled away from the place where he was to meet the agents. Each second seemed painful and tiring as he would look over his shoulder until he reached a decrepit building.

He walked past the front and turned into, and alleyway. The next second, he climbed through a loose window and entered the building without delay. He knew this was no accident and that his life would be in danger anyway. He simply chose to defy the inevitable outcome of that place and the loss of his family. John needed to defy these agents and the torture tactics that had been used in his state of being. He had spent the last eight years running from those events. Now, he would take matters into his own hands.

He quickly moved across the floor of the building to a garage door on the far side. With the unlocking of a few latches, he slid the door up as quietly as he could manage, then walked the short distance to an old Ford Lightning that seemed to wait for him. He turned the key and seemed satisfied when the engine sounded without hesitation. One pull on the shifting arm, and he was rolling out of the building and onto the tight streets of New York City.

Little time had passed until he crossed the bridge into New Jersey and continued onward. John knew that his only option lay in West Virginia, and he hoped that the journey would lead him to salvation. The agents would follow, and he knew this as one of them had tipped him off. It was the man who accompanied them and always stood in the lobby of the building.

He was always examining a map on the wall, and it was only the last time that John noticed the map's content. Push pins dotted the area around Fairmont and seemed to have some importance. Nothing could tell John anything that he didn't already know at that moment. This investigation was about more than someone recounting their lives and the horrors they had witnessed. Though it seemed the agents may struggle to catch him before arriving in West Virginia.

It had never been stated that he had been paying the taxes and mortgage until its end. There was no doubt that the old house stood in ruins now as no one had been able to live there since. The raw state that John was in meant that he would drive nearly continuously to West Virginia. Nothing could stop him or get in his way now. His mental and emotional state leaned on the conclusion to it all. The states now flew past as he reached the Maryland and West Virginia border.

Harper's Ferry lay a short distance from him now as night had taken the land once more. John pulled into a gas station to refuel and stretch his legs. He stepped out of the truck and again placed the gun in its concealed holster. He walked inside the store and handed cash to the attendant.

"Thank you, sir. Long drive?"

"It has been, but I have a short time now until I'm there."

"Where is there, sir? If I may ask."

"Fairmont, West Virginia"

The look he gave the attendant seemed to unsettle the guy. He just handed John his change and told him to have a good night. Surely the legend of Fairmont had not finally escaped the town. None of that mattered now as John slid the gas nozzle into his truck and clicked the lock down.

He heard the pump click again and pulled the nozzle from the gas tank. He felt the hose lock into the side of the pump as he turned and placed the gas cap back into its position.

"Mr. Dorsett, where are you going?"

John looked around him frantically, but saw no one around.

Before John knew it, he was back on the highway and heading into West Virginia as quickly as he could. He had not heard the voice for some time, but he could not be sure they weren't inside his head. Could it be that he had finally gone insane from these events and being forced to live within them again? He had not been called to think about these events for some time, and it seemed unhealthy to do so. John was not a man who would reach out to a therapist or such professionals for the help that he could give himself.

The horrors of Fairmont had been pushed from his life every day since he had left the area. Those memories had never come to him unless he were alone and thinking about it. Sometimes, that little pull on his heart forced him to recall the pain and emotion of it all. The look on Jeanette's face as she suffered in silence around him. The terror that had overcome his children each time that these entities would attack.

This was the only thing that he was called to remember until these agents began their investigation. At that time, he felt compelled to cooperate with them, but this was not his desire. It was as though he had become possessed by some force that compelled his mind to cooperate with them. The only thing that seemed to free him was the torment that his heart and soul had endured. This would change now, and he would finally end what had started all that time ago.

Finally, he crossed into Morgantown and began the drive to Fairmont. It seemed that time had begun to pull him in one direction, and he would never be able to escape. He was focused on other things to throw the voices off his trail and toward Florida. The focus was on retirement within the sunshine and beaches that Florida had offered him. However, he was not sure that those days would come anytime soon. The fear would be that he would be trapped in New York forever as the agents may never allow him to leave.

The night now seemed to be a mirror that reflected his life to him. He could see the alignment of stars just in the same way that he could so long ago. The nights of sitting on the porch and looking up into the heavens now flooded his mind. He tried to think of other things, but it seemed to get the better of him. However, there seemed to be a calm and healing sensation from this. John sped down I-68 toward 76 as he turned on some music but heard nothing but silence.

Every station seemed drowned out except for one that played an eerie orchestral sound. He listened for a moment as his skin began to crawl from that sound until it was broken by a loud "Eeeeeeeeeee" sound that came through the speakers. This all turned to a woman speaking numbers and names through the speakers and seemed to grow louder. This had taken over every channel now, and no matter how far he would turn the dial, the sound was the same. Yet the voice had grown to be multiple women saying the same thing at the same time. Then the station went silent, bringing back the eerie music again.

He felt it prudent to turn the radio off and give up the search for music. Instead, John pushed the gas pedal deeper into the floorboard while listening to the powerful 351 roar to life again. Before he knew what was going on, he was over 100MPH and climbing. The interstate was empty and seemed to have no other vehicles except the occasional semi. The air outside the truck grew louder as John rolled his window down and felt the chill of the night wafting into his truck.

Fall was alive in West Virginia, just as it was when he experienced the bulk of the sightings. This season, John would depart West Virginia for many years. However, it seemed that settling this all once and for all was the only freedom that John would taste in many years. Still, he had many things to do before he could enter that home again. Somehow, he knew what he must do at each step as if being spoken to by another entity.

Fairmont quickly approached as he continued to hammer on the gas. This last stretch of lone darkness seemed to put him outside the range of whatever had been affecting him. His affliction had ended, and his mind seemed at ease again. The world seemed to change, and the pressure that he had felt to return to his apartment immediately subsided. Perhaps it was true that these agents were using his mind as a communication device to control his impulses.

If this were true, then John would no longer be the man crumpled in the corner, sobbing to himself while these freaks stared at him. They weren't human in nature, and everything told him that now. They had no emotion, nor did they seem to ever be in the sun as their skin was almost translucent. Yet they seemed normal in every other aspect but still off to his senses. Then, there was the smell of rotting flesh that would emanate from them but only briefly, which John still could not understand.

The night was invaded by light from Fairmont just before him as he came over a hill and began descending toward the town. He would leave the interstate and cross the bridge that took him to town. Ultimately, it was the Super 8 that welcomed him into the town and into sleep as he locked everything and pulled the blinds shut. His mind raced as he slipped into unconsciousness and then passed into his dreams. There was no care in the world at that moment and only the cool sheets could comfort him as he lay in the darkness of the early morning hours.

7

The morning was in full swing by the time he awoke from his deep rest. Something had begun to comfort his soul as he was rested beyond anything he had felt in years. He was no longer forced to dream while being called into torment within his mind. John didn't feel like a shell floating through life any longer and now seemed alive again. That was until the phone began to ring in his room.

He lifted the receiver from the rocker and placed it on his ear.

"Hello?"

"Sorry to bother you, Mr. Dorsett, but you have a call from someone claiming to know you."

"Yes. Put them through, please."

A slightly gruff voice with a commanding tone came over the line.

"John? You back in town? One of my friends at the department called me this morning saying that you were back. Is this true?"

"Sheriff, I don't want any shit, but yeah...it's true."

"I told you that it would infect your mind. Shame what happened, but it's only natural to end up where you started. Come find me at Mom's Place on Hoult Street."

"Understood, Sheriff."

The line went dead and was silent again. With a click, John placed the receiver back on the rocker and began preparing to meet the sheriff. Without hesitation, he left his room and locked it up behind him.

John met the sheriff in a booth in the far corner only to be poured a cup of coffee and placed an order for eggs and sausage.

"Why the hell would you want to come back, John?"

"I don't know, but something tells me my life will be better when I face this. I've been under investigation by some group who just call themselves agents. They look legit enough, but I question it now. I have suffered through some of what happened and the pain, but it won't go away. They won't stop harassing me, and I finally got a call from Jeanette."

The sheriff's face went white as he placed his hand over his heart. Nothing could have prepared him for such words, and he seemed deeply troubled by them.

"I am sorry, John. This seems to have gotten out of hand. Trust me when I say that you don't want to be here. The activity is going on again, as you know."

"I don't have a choice now, sheriff. I am lost in this, and I need to end it now. Do you know where all of this started? Where the first sightings were?"

John's food hit the table as he thanked the waitress. The eggs and sausage steamed and gave off a freshness he had not smelled in some time. The quality of food in New York City was not what it used to be. It seemed fake at times, but this tingled all of the senses with each bite.

"I can tell you, but not here. You up for a drive?"

John simply nodded with a serious look on his face.

"Then lay low until tonight. If they see us going to that place, then we will be stopped. We will take my car as they know me and won't question anything. You say nothing at all. If they find out, then you and I will be killed to keep the secret."

With those words, the old cop stood up and tipped his hat to the waitress. John ate in silence, only to stare at the sheriff's ticket, which was covered in money. Even John's food was on the list as another favor from the man who felt responsible for his suffering.

Silence seemed to fill the diner completely as time passed and customers came and went. John finished his eggs and stood from the table to leave. The waitress and staff seemed to stare at him as he did.

He knew the whole town would know what happened to the man with the black truck's family. Many wouldn't know his name or any deeds he had committed then. He was a nobody within the town again and liked it that way. It wouldn't stop the murmurs from towns-folk nor the people around him who would look upon his face. Surely, his story had been added to the legend of this town by now. John just pushed it out of his mind as he got back in the truck and lit a cigarette.

He took a long drag only to contemplate this town's horrors and the secrets it hides. How would he come to terms with the torment of his family and the loss of connection that they felt? Nothing could tell him now other than waiting for the ex-sheriff to find him at the Super 8. He had pondered if he should have told the man where he would be, but he was sure he would be found when it was time.

The only thing left was to get inside and hide himself as best he could. He was forced to park in a different place and walk from the Cracker Barrel to his room. He knew these agents would stop at nothing to find him before he could interfere. However how long that would take was subjective. He rushed into his room once more and locked everything he could. The TV was the only sound that he could hear other than the occasional person leaving their room and walking around.

The world then would fall silent again as he continued to rest and wait. Time passed quickly until he noticed that the sun had begun to fall behind the horizon once more. At that moment, a knock came from the other side of the door, followed by:

"Open the door! It's time to go."

The voice was that of the sheriff calling for the time to leave again. John followed him silently to his crown vic, and then the men departed the Super 8. The drive was long and uneventful until they reached a small dirt road that ran off to the left of the main road.

They drove down it slowly with the spotlights on the sheriff's car activated and actively looking about.

This night was different in this place as the light of the stars and moon did not seem to reach into this void. The woods around the road were silent, and only the feeling of the chill in the air let John know they were still on planet Earth. There came a sound over the radio like a clicking noise as the sheriff turned off his lights and continued to the end of the road. This ended at a lake with an old house sitting in the silent darkness.

"This is the first place we know of all this happening. That house was built long ago before anyone settled these lands. It was a lot smaller back then, but now shows the renovations of later inhabitants. I don't know if this always happened here or started in the early 1800's. The only thing we do know is that these events continue to this day and seemed to start here."

"How did you find that out?"

"You don't get it, Mr. Dorsett. This is a file that is maintained by the sheriff's office in town. Every sheriff is brought into this world and then taken to this house. It's like a damned initiation at this point. No one could explain why it happened or when it would stop, but that doesn't matter now. I have lost people to this shit and while others might not care, I do. I take the protection of this area and its citizens seriously."

"Do you know how to stop it?"

"No one does. But we might find something to answer that inside. Come on!"

The two men exited the car and began walking cautiously. Toward the decrepit home. Their flashlights shined light just enough to get a feel for where they were going, but the whole area seemed to swallow light more than usual. The trees hung over the entryway to the home and all around the area. John and the sheriff could see nothing in the way of a door anymore as the bushes had grown up around the property. The shadows seemed to shift within the home rapidly.

It appeared that the darkness would shift forms and dart from area to area as if waiting for the men to enter. John had crept close to a window on the first level and peered through to see the outline of something pale standing at the edge of his light. It seemed to hide itself in the darkness, but in a way so that John was unsure what he was witnessing. Just then, he was touched on his left shoulder as he jumped back and yelled out as quietly as he could.

"Follow me! We are going in through the basement and then into the house. I don't know what is inside, but I don't like the sounds that I am hearing."

John nodded back at the sheriff as they walked around the building and into the basement. Both men reached the doorway of the basement and slowly crept inside. The darkness swirled about like a mist on the wind, then seemed to form temporary shapes and forms on the edge of their vision. Neither man said anything, but the looks that they shared communicated enough. They continued forward slowly until they reached the stairs to the first floor.

The upper levels creaked slowly and methodically, almost as if someone were pacing and waiting on the men. The night outside changed as John peered through another window as the light of lightning flashed all around the area. When he turned back to the sheriff at the top of the stairs, shapes and forms seemed to be reflected in the flashes at brief moments. The sheriff waved John forward, and he moved quickly and silently up the stairs.

Both men emerged on the first floor and began looking about in the rooms of the home. The kitchen and the living room were only divided by a bar and counter that seemed built to entertain and serve guests. Though it was not the same type that a full-service bar would contain. The living room still held recliners and a large wrap-around sofa that was all set into the floor on a lower level. The last inhabitants seemed to have left sometime in the 60's.

The carpet was crimson, and the walls were a dirty cream color, which both seemed to have rotted slightly while sitting in this area. The fascinating revelation was that trees and bushes had nearly covered the outside but the inside seemed pristine. No windows had been broken, and the floors seemed sturdy enough to walk upon comfortably. This was all odd until the sound of screaming emanated from somewhere above and nearly sent both men to the floor.

John shot behind a recliner as the sheriff pulled his .357 magnum. Eventually, they regrouped in the kitchen only to whisper to one another.

"What the hell was that?"

"I don't know, but it reminds me of my own home."

"Do you have a gun?"

John nodded.

"Good. Pull that son of a bitch and use it if you have to. Just don't shoot me in the back."

John nodded again, then followed the sheriff to the doorway that led up to the second floor.

John went first, with Sheriff Barkley just behind. They both moved as a tight-knit unit to the top landing and then started to look through the rooms on each side of the hallway. John entered the room on the right as Sheriff Barkley went to the left. Just as John had entered the room, the sound of pitter-pattering feet ran past the doorway behind him. He froze in fear as a small giggle emanated from the stairs just beyond the wall. He could only turn and wait for anything that might enter the room with him.

He wasn't sure, but it seemed as though the sheriff noticed nothing. Just then, the door to the closet deeper inside the room flew open, and another Child's laughter could be heard. This was accompanied by footsteps running past John and out into the hallway. His blood ran cold instantly, and he refused to move for a moment. The air around him as the thing passed became icy and difficult to breathe.

Thunder and lighting crashed all around the outside of the home, increasing as the men moved deeper into the home. That was when John noticed that he was standing in a child's room, which seemed to be a little boy's. There were familiar toys that he knew from his own childhood in the 70's. Though some things seemed older, especially the wooden bed that had begun to rot and fall apart. However, there were additions to the room, such as blood spatters.

John left that room and moved down the hall to the next, only to enter a teenage girl's room. He entered the doorway only to be overcome with the stench of rotting meat. Just then, he looked to the right to see a withered and rotted corpse of the girl sitting up on the bed. She was looking right at him with haunting recesses where her eyes had been, and the smell was awful. Blood had pooled on the ground under her as she sat naked with some tissue coming from inside her and down underneath the bed.

He dared not look under the bed and stepped back out of the room. John refused to turn his back on that room as the image of the girl in what seemed like a birthing position haunted him. God only knows what was under the bed, but he felt it was likely her baby. How she had come to be that way after birth was of question, but he refused to give it a voice. Suddenly, a pop of thunder came sharply and seemed to split the sky in two. This was followed by silence again broken by the crying of a baby.

Neither man could explain the sound, but it seemed to grow louder like the creature was coming closer. Yet the fear rooted them in place, and they could not run from the sound or even speak. There was no control over their bodies other than this deep fear that rang through their veins. The eventual conclusion was to begin hearing the sounds of tiny hands smacking slowly against the wooden floors and even a deformed head peering around the corner and into the hallway.

The head was crushed inward on the right side, along with one eye-rolling across the ground and half of the jaw missing. Nothing could explain how this profane child could move or even produce the crying sounds. With another crash of thunder the event had ended as though nothing had peered around the corner. The sounds also ended without any understanding of this event.

John and the sheriff looked at each other and then forced themselves to move toward the end of the hall and up the stairs to the next level. The screaming came in a second wave as their footsteps moved closer to the upper landing. The sound reverberated through everything around them until it seemed to collide with both men and push them back. John caught himself by the railing of the stairs and managed to keep from falling back into the hallway. They pressed on slowly and cautiously as they reached the top and began looking around.

This level seemed to be turning back on itself and leading the men to only three rooms that were now on their right. The wooden floors now creaked in an eerie and altogether unsettling way as they pressed on. John searched the nearest room while the sheriff moved into the next. Both rooms seemed to be completely empty, with the outlining of furniture that had been removed for one reason or another.

Though the windows had been covered and sealed for some strange reason. The stench of the home now faded and left the only scent to be mildew and rot from the roof above. Water seemed to pool on top of the ceiling just above a shared closet. The ceiling within the closet had rotted away long ago and left an empty void of darkness. The oddest impression was that neither room held access to the attic above.

There seemed to be ample space for an attic but no way to access it other than a possible hatch in the last room. John pondered this as Sheriff Barkley continued looking about the room where he stood. Nothing else seemed to be out of place, and the rooms continued their silence. John moved back toward the door and began pulling at the fabric nailed over the window in this room.

He could not seem to manage the removal of this cloth. There should be no reason to cover the windows unless they were broken and an attempt to seal them had been made. A most troubling sound could be heard just as he began to cut at the cloth with his pocket knife. The stairs had begun creaking and shifting as if someone were walking up them.

Each step grew louder than the last until the final few steps were left. John spun himself to face the door and witnessed the top of a woman's head barely poking above the railing. He gasped as he realized what was going on until the form moved forward again and took its place on the top landing. It was the corpse of the girl that was rotting on the floor below. She was moving slowly and in jerky motions, as she approached him.

Her moaning seemed to fill the room until John noticed that the thing hanging from her was an umbilical cord with her baby still attached. The baby seemed to be drug along as its head bumped over the boards that made up the flooring. John panicked and pulled his gun, only to hear more powerful shots coming from the other room.

He lifted the gun and approached the door as he fired shot after shot into the body. The girl groaned, and the sounds of her becoming aroused followed. She had begun to moan loudly as if being in a state of intense pleasure. It could not be possible that this thing could move less that she could haunt this home in such a state. Eventually, a shot rang out that went through the corpse's skull and blew her head apart. It was the .357 magnum that finished her off at point-blank range. Her body dropped into the doorway where John had approached as he shifted into the attached room.

He now followed the sheriff forward and toward the final room. The door seemed stuck as both men began to ram the door with their shoulders. The door seemed anchored into the wall firmly and held little rot. It also did not give as an old door should in a crumbling home. Eventually, John used his gun to bash the lock off and kick the door in. The sheriff immediately rushed into the room and began checking the corners.

John followed this process until they realized that something was not right. There seemed to be a soft surface under their feet as they stood within the pitch-black space. There came a flash of lightning that was followed by a loud thunder that shook the house and rolled across the land. The light showed a flash of the room, which seemed to show people nailed to the walls. John flicked the flashlight on only to recoil in disgust.

There were four people nailed to walls, one on each wall, that seemed to be positioned in a profane way. Each had been placed in the crucifixion position while having their eyes and tongues removed. Each corpse seemed fresh and in no way seemed to have rotted over the time they were there. A loud crash came from behind a door that seemed to separate another room from this one. The sheriff moved to open that door as the bodies upon the wall had begun to convulse. Their heads animated, and immediately began following the sheriff as he approached the door.

John was horrified at this sight but continued to cover the sheriff and wait. Eventually, the sound of a clicking lock could be heard, followed by the door opening from within. There were patterns across the floor and walls in the blood that held itself in its original shape. This defied all logic to John as he could not begin to process what he was witnessing. How could all of this be possible?

The sheriff left the room he had just entered and urged John to run for the basement.

"Let's get the fuck out of here, John!"

Both men rushed past the body of the young girl and her baby and then down the stairs. The image of this place was clear now to the sheriff, but John could not understand what he had witnessed.

Both men made it out of the house and back to the car as intense screaming came from behind them. Crashing thunder sounded all around and shook the windows of the car. Sheriff Barkley started his car and turned on his lights as the lanky bastard that had haunted John appeared. There arose an anger within him that he could not ignore, but he tried his best to fight the urge to shoot this thing. The car raced down the road and back out onto the main highway.

8

The storm immediately subsided as soon as they had reached the city's limits once more. Both men said nothing until they reached the comfort of Petie's Pub. They moved quickly inside and ordered a Johnnie Walker on the rocks each. The scotch went down smoothly. Then the sheriff paused and looked at John.

"What in the hell happened in that place? I don't understand what kind of devil shit could be going on there. I know that everything started long before that upper floor had been built, so how in the hell did anyone live with that?"

John stared forward and across the bar.

"There were guts and blood all over the floor. They were tied to the bodies on the walls. What in the actual fuck happened in there?"

The sheriff mumbled something, then took a long sip of his scotch.

"There are no words to describe what I think happened, but I don't want to say. Does it give life to evil to speak on evil?"

"I don't know, John. I see why only one sheriff in the area's history had the balls to walk into that God-forsaken place. I just hope God can help those souls in that place."

John followed the sheriff's words by performing the cross sign that connected his head, stomach and shoulders together. They said nothing more until John was being dropped off at his hotel.

"Be careful, John! Something will know that we went into that place, and you will be a target."

John nodded and thanked the sheriff as he entered his room and locked the door immediately.

The sheriff had urged him to hold onto the pistol and even provided another ammo magazine. He placed them on the bedside table and began checking around the room. Nothing seemed to be out of place, and no corpses followed him to his room. Just in case, he pulled a crucifix from his bag and placed it on the bed beside him as he slept.

The night passed quickly and without issue, other than the occasional sound from outside waking him. His mind seemed to be empty in anticipation for some monster to crawl through his room and murder him. John had thought that the events that haunted his Fairmont home disturbed him, but it was only a pale comparison to what was in that house. The most disturbing to him was the corpse of the young girl. Nothing could describe the images of the face in his mind, and it seemed there every time he closed his eyes.

The sounds of a crying baby seemed to echo through his mind when he was alone, so he left the room as soon as he could get ready himself. The intent was to head to Cracker Barrel and eat a hearty and hot meal. He thought of his family as he ate in the dining area's lonely corner. The waitress did little to change this as she seemed to remind him of his ex-wife. Surely it was all just a coincidence rather than a meaningful attack upon his psyche.

The way that all of this would function was an enigma to John, and he knew no other way to be about it. The terror would not leave him as his mind had been scarred by the intense fear and horrid images. He could only eat quickly and leave for another bar across town. He sat down before obtaining the name of the place and immediately ordered a beer and a shot.

"A shot at 11 AM?"

"I've had a rough couple of days."

John pulled out a pocket full of cash and held it out for the bartender to see. The woman just placed the shot on the counter. John immediately inhaled it and then washed it down with a sip of his beer. He now knew how all the troubled heroes in the movies had come to drink so intensely. John could now understand the importance of drinking to forget.

He sat at the bar and thought about his family and beautiful wife. Everything about that time seemed to point at a troubled woman and a man who struggled to save his family. The thoughts brought him to tears before everyone, only for him to begin drinking faster and faster until he collapsed on the bar. Time passed slowly as he drifted from his current space and back to those days.

He could see and feel everything happy about his family in those early days. John was a broken man who struggled to find the pieces of himself that had been left behind rather than putting them in place. Nothing seemed to fix him at all, and he couldn't even understand how to begin. He prayed every day of his life and still suffered through the most despair. The loss of his children, however, was too much for him to think about.

They had all been taken away by these entities and had grown as distant as they could from him. Only pictures within his apartment remained to remind him of the good and bad memories that would haunt him forever. He felt the creeping sensation of misery looming on the edge of his thoughts. He could not allow it all to flood in and take him over, but he had no way to alleviate himself of it.

The darkness seemed to be too much to cope with at certain points, and this was no different. Now he was too deep in the shit to change his course of action from facing these entities. His only thought was to change the world in which these beings inhabited. To save anyone else who would venture into the area.

It wasn't from a position of nobility but more from a space of longing for peace in his life and the lives of all who live near Fairmont. West Virginia had always been presented as a haunted state, but now seemed more cursed. Nothing could have prepared him for this time in his life, and every moment brought him closer to its conclusion. The only thing that would make this all worse is to attract any agents to the area to find him.

These thoughts gave him a sense of hurry and impatience, but he could not allow himself to go into this unprepared. Yet now, all he could do was sit and drink at the altar of despair. All of this forever tainted his soul, and he felt trapped within this world.

Eventually, he would have another round followed immediately by another, but nothing brought him any peace. He could no longer feel his mind or even his face, for that matter. John was lost in the darkness that threatened to take him away from the world and into eternity. Could he embrace its message and give in to this evil? His mind held firm in the negative on that opinion.

Nothing in John's life could have prepared him for witnessing the terror of it all, but it was clear that something had been allowed to infect the area. The powers that be that protected it seemed all too able to allow for the corruption of the land and its people. The world seemed dimer than anyone could understand unless they had dealt with such evil.

It was becoming clearer with every sip that John had been called upon to end the terrors of the area, but he was unsure how to start. Any mistake, at this point in time, could prevent anything from changing. It seemed that no one else would be able to affect change within the wilds around Fairmont. There was little that could change the outcome of what had happened already, but it would solve the problem for the future.

This was when John Dorsett put his mind to solving the problem. The thought that came to mind was seeing himself burning the building to the ground. Through fire, the evils that had been done within that structure could be cleansed and purified. He had no idea how he had come to that revelation, but it seemed as good as any.

He stood from the bar after a second whiskey shot and put on his jacket. John paid the tab and left without another word or pause. He hopped into his truck and left for the sheriff's office in town. He could not waste any time in letting the sheriff know about his plans.

However, he was sure that Sheriff Barkley would take issue with returning to the place.

The memory of the directions had been burned within John's mind forever, giving him no excuse to falter on his plans. He pulled into the station's parking lot and entered the building shortly after. The deputy at the desk didn't even ask his name or why he wished to speak with the sheriff. She just pointed to her left and asked him to wait by the door. John did as she asked, taking his seat in the first chair beside the doorway.

The time seemed to slow, and every minute seemed like an eternity as he sat in the chair and read a magazine. Just as he had turned to the place in the magazine he wished to read, the door opened, and Sheriff Barkley motioned for him to enter. He then spoke to the clerk to hold any calls and ask for people to wait before entering.

John now sat before the sheriff within an office that many a criminal would not wish to see. Sheriff, I have a plan to rid the area of this mess, but I need your help. Would you give me that help? The sheriff looked about for a moment and nodded but did not speak. I will go to that place and bring fire to the structure from within that alter room.

The sheriff looked at him with an odd face being made that John could not place. It was as if these words brought pain to the sheriff, but still nothing was said. He simply closed his eyes and creased his lips together as if the pain had worsened within his body.

"I cannot advise going there again. They know we went there, but not any details of the visit. I told them you were helping me secure the area and ensure everything was alright. It was the only way to keep them from coming for us both."

John said nothing.

"Going back there would be an issue in every sense of the word. You're going to get yourself and me killed. They don't like the idea of losing a hold over this place."

"Sheriff, who are "they"?"

"I will not say anything more on that topic. You don't understand the deep shit that you're bringing upon us. I don't have anything that could start something like that anyway. Flares would be ineffective, and I have no more in the trunk of my car. You also are out of luck because my car is locked, and to enter that vehicle would be theft of public property."

John understood this line of thinking perfectly and began formulating a plan.

"Just stay the hell out of this, sir. I don't want you getting involved in this otherwise, you'll be killed, and I'll have to kill you. Sacrifices must be made on the alter to protect this place."

John looked directly into Sheriff Barkley's eyes and replied, "I won't do anything to endanger the public then. Sorry to bother you, sheriff. I don't like that you're protecting this place, but that is between you and God at this point."

John then stood, left the sheriff's station, and drove back to his motel room on the other side of town. The gears now turned within his mind, bringing images of the steps needed to complete such an action. He did not understand everything he had been called to do, but he would not argue. Instead, he simply rested in the room with the curtains drawn while watching TV until 6 PM.

He was compelled to perform additional steps that would assist, or so he thought. John drove to the local Catholic Church and entered. He had never been within this church, but he recognized its importance within this place. The name had been given to St. Peter the Fisherman, and he knew the importance of such a place being involved.

John entered quietly and genuflected before taking a seat in the pew and beginning to pray. He opened his mind to the thoughts of the universe within this place as the sign of the cross was motioned over his forehead. He had now become one with God in this holy place and bared his mind before the Lord. He could immediately feel a passion taking him over as well as his burdens lifting from his shoulders.

Mr. Dorsett was no longer blaming himself for all that had happened, as the eyes of the Lord had seen him within such strife. He felt cleansed within the placing of himself within the church. It had been too long since he had come to the church for anything, but it could not be more clear that he had been accepted. After all, he was born within the church and taught within New York City.

It was natural that no one seemed to inhabit this place and no one approached him. A priest went about his duties within this space and seemed to not notice John as he continued to pray and bear his soul. Now, all had been taken from him, and his mind had been eased. In its place, he could feel empowered and healed. His body no longer ached, and his vision became clearer as he continued.

Upon opening his eyes, John was a free man with a clear mind about what he needed to do for this area to be made right. Though he could not see any solution in which he would be left alive after all was said and done. Sweat began to pool on his forehead and drip down to his brow as he wiped it away. Just then, a voice began to speak to him that he did not know.

"Those distressed in this world shall wield the purifying flame to such evil. You are blessed within the eyes of the Lord. I know nothing about what you will do, but I can understand its importance. Have faith that the world will be purified in His name upon your passing."

The priest then bowed slightly and made the sign of the cross over John. "May you be blessed in the name of the Father, Son, and Holy Spirit".

This ended the interaction as the priest left John's side and began going about his duties again. John saw this as a clear sign and left the church. He had a clear image in his mind of what he must do and began his plan immediately. John parked is truck just near the station, but not around the station. He then walked over to the sheriff's car and began pulling on the driver's door.

The door opened immediately as John slipped inside and started it with the spare key left in the cup holder. He backed out of the space and drove off without anyone attempting to stop him. John took this as ultimate confirmation that this plan was for the betterment of the world. He drove out of town and turned onto the lonely country road that took him to the soft dirt road the sheriff had taken down the previous night.

It was not long until the world around him had changed again to the storms that raged and the dark woods surrounding it. Time sped up, and it seemed as though he had not gone nearly as far of a distance to the house. After switching off the engine, John rushed from the car and opened the trunk to retrieve a shotgun and ammo. He then pulled a flare from the spare compartment and placed them within the waist of his pants.

He moved as quickly as he could into the house and rushed the stairs to the second level. This was all stopped by the emergence of the bodies of people in the upper room. John shucked a bullet into the chamber and pulled the trigger repeatedly. Holes were blown through the bodies, which left bits of rotten flesh scattering the walls. He moved forward cautiously as he pumped each shot into the bodies until nothing was left moving.

He took the steps to the upper level and backed himself into the corner again. As swift as he could, John reloaded the shotgun and shucked another round into the chamber. He took the time to make the sign of the cross and thank God for delivering him from this evil. Only a glance gave him the realization that the house held no bodies as the carnage had vanished. He wished to think about this but thought it better to move forward.

9

John stood again and moved cautiously past the two rooms on the right of the third floor until he reached the last door. He could not manage to make the door open nor would it give to repeated kicks. This didn't make any sense as the door had easily been opened the night before, but nothing seemed to make it move. He did not wish to level a shot through the lock as he felt that this would not work.

As he thought about his next moves, John could feel something wrap around his waist and begin tugging on him. He looked down to see beautiful and gentle hands begin to rub their way up him. Though they were not the hands that he had imagined to be there. No, these were beautiful hands that were perfectly shaped and made that were covered in the softest, chocolate-colored skin.

His mind could not fathom that Jeanette had arrived at this place, and he knew this was all within his mind, but he could not understand how. Just then he felt someone bring their lips to his left ear and whisper into it.

"I have missed you, John. I am sorry that I never said goodbye and that we never really worked out. I blame myself for that baby. Stop what you're doing and come to me, my love."

He stopped what he was doing and closed his eyes as he began to absorb the feeling of his ex-wife's embrace. It was soft and gentle, yet inviting to him, and without pause, he turned to see her there before him. Her afro wafted in the wind just the way he liked it. Her ample curves were only covered in a tiny red thong and bra set that had always driven him crazy.

John fell into her embrace as she kissed his neck and around to his lips until she reached down and grasped his crotch. Her other arm had reached out and began removing the shotgun from his hand.

"Don't leave me again, baby. I cannot bear to think of my life without you, John."

She motioned for him to look at her beautiful breasts and luscious hips.

"Do you want me tonight, John? I'm all yours. I'll do anything to make this all up to you, baby."

Nothing could begin to make sense at this moment, but John could not stop it until he felt the motion of movement from the place he had stood. He closed his eyes and opened them again to see that he was staring up at the ceiling, and Jeanette was no longer standing before him.

Instead, he had been lifted from the ground and turned to look upward toward the ceiling. Though he could still feel the grasp around his waist, it was no longer that of his wife. He looked down to see a tentacle wrapped around him that ended in a spike. The spike had been plunged deep within his belly button, but no pain emanated from this place on his body.

John began to struggle as he realized that he was being pulled into the hole in the ceiling. Whatever this creature was, he could not tell, but he had become determined to struggle against it. The shotgun had been removed from his hand and was lying upon the ground where he had just stood. John worked his hand into his pants pocket and pulled out his knife.

The pain then began to pulse from his belly button and was immense. He had become nearly crippled by the pain as he began stabbing the tentacle quickly and as hard as he could. The force of the stabbing allowed the spike to be removed from him as he screamed out in pain. A black liquid had begun flowing from the wounds on the creature as it dropped him to the floor below. John dove to the ground and grabbed the shotgun only to pump a round through the ceiling.

He then shucked another cartridge into the chamber and immediately fired. He did this rapidly over and over until the tentacles that hung from the hold in the ceiling went limp and hung from the hold. John loaded another few cartridges into the shotgun from the box that he had brought from the car. He then pumped another three rounds into the exact same spot in the ceiling.

There was no motion from the tentacles in that moment, and he relegated the thing to being slain. This was when he had begun searching around from another way into that room. Though he did not think to check the door again. Instead, he climbed into the ceiling and pulled his way around the creature's body within this darkness. John could see a light that shined from the floor in a corner of this place.

He pulled himself along the flooring and to the light, then looked through the hole. It was the room where the bodies had been hung on the walls, but it seemed bright and empty now. He could not understand this as the home seemed normal now. He reached down and flipped himself through the hole. A loud thud could be heard throughout the structure, with his landing within the room.

The room seemed light all around, with sunshine coming through the blinds and filtering into the room. The commotion of a TV playing somewhere in the house and people talking could be heard. It seemed the room had been painted in a bright blue that reminded him of a nursery, but no furniture reinforced this.

The room had been found bare but was clean and inhabited by no horrors John could detect. He walked quietly across the floor as he brought the shotgun to bear on the door that led to the altar. He reached out and pulled the door open suddenly then prepared for something to emerge. His finger rested upon the trigger lightly but to pull it. The room beyond the door was normal, however, and showed no signs of the blood that had made that horrible pattern all around. No alter was set within this room, and no indication had been made that there was ever anything like that within this space.

For all he could know, John had been placed within another world to protect the alter from harm, but this was only a guess. John lowered the shotgun and wondered what to do next. How had he been pulled into this place and could he return? He moved back into the other room and looked around, but no hole could be seen. It was as if he were firmly within this other world with no way out.

He could only wonder about the horror below him in the heart of the home. By all indications, however, the world was renewed in this time period as the outside seemed beautiful and tranquil. Just then, John could hear someone moving up the stairs to this level and toward the room in which he stood. He panicked but could find no place to hide as nothing could conceal him from sight.

Instead, he crept back into the other room and place himself in the closet with the shotgun, ready to kill anything that presented harm. Now the footsteps had multiplied into multiple feet moving through the doorway and into the room he had just crept from. They entered the room just beyond the closet door, and the people stood in a half circle.

They each seemed to be in a trance as they simply stared at the place where the alter would come to be. One stepped forward and was a girl of sixteen. She held her hands up to the light and led the rest in a change that John could not understand. The language was not of anything he had heard before, but seemed ominous none-theless. Just then, the girl spoke in English as she commanded the void to enter her body and gift her a child.

She commanded an entity whose name sounded awful and held a gurgling sound within the syllables. The girl then turned and spoke to the family as she commanded that she was to be impregnated by this entity.

"I will bear the darkened one into this world through my body. I will be gifted the love of peace through the cosmic void."

The rest of the family bowed before her and spoke in that strange language again. The girl stepped forward, grasped her father's hand, and led him away.

The thought of what would come next seemed burned within John's mind as he could hear the footsteps moving toward the second level. Immediately, he put the bits of information together and knew that it was her father who had impregnated her. She had come to bear the child that he had seen still attached to her rotting corpse.

How could a parent be complicit in the defilement of their own daughter in this way? John's stomach turned as he forced the thoughts from his mind and willed them away. He looked again to see that no one was in the room again. A silence had fallen over the house save for the sound of the TV again.

He crept from the closet as he looked around to make sure that no one was waiting for him to leave. He crept out into the other room only to notice that the son of the family had been killed and stuck to that wall. The boy didn't seem to be any older than six, as his intestines and blood had been strewn across the floor. John blinked and opened his eyes again to see that now the wife had been done the same way. She had been impaled to the wall directly in front of him as she was gutted and bled out all the same.

What sick people would do this to their family? John once again pushed the thought from his mind as he dared not contemplate such evil. Instead, he made the sign of the cross and continued onward. He then crept from this room and toward the stairs. The sounds of people having sex could be heard now as he crept down the stairs slowly.

His stomach again turned as he knew what he was about to witness. He paused on the stairs and tried to wait it out as he had no desire to see this despicable act. Instead, the sounds continued on and on until he could no longer take it. He peeked into the room to see the sixteen-year-old girl riding atop her father as they both moaned together.

Eventually, they both came to a final climax, and John began to throw up in his mouth. He wished for it all to end so badly that he leaped into the room and pumped a round into both of them. Yet nothing changed, and they continued on as if he were not present. He was forced to witness them embrace and kiss over and over until they started again.

He closed his eyes to shield his psyche, but the sounds immediately stopped. He could not understand why this was all being shown to him. When he opened his eyes again, the girl sat on her father's lap. She was now pregnant and seemed to be happy that she had fallen into such a horrible sin. Her body seemed odd, though, as her veins looked like black lines on a map that connected together.

Her skin was now a milky white and her eyes were blazing red. What manner of evil was this that he witnessed? He blinked again, only to see the girl naked on the edge of her bed. She had her legs spread and was pleasuring herself until blood and fluid evacuated her. She began screaming in pain as her father entered the room. He had a small sickle-like implement within his right hand.

The girl began screaming louder and louder as the sounds of a baby emerging from her could be heard. Her father stood in front of her and had clearly begun to fondle her. This all continued until the baby crawled from within her and up her torso. It began suckling from her as the father slit her throat, and the blood ran down over the child. This seemed to cause spider legs to emerge from the infant's back. The sight was unimaginably horrid as John struggled to watch. The child reached out its hand, and the father took it from the room.

The naked girl sat on the edge of the bed as the blood pooled beneath her on the floor. The umbilical cord stretched down and under the bed slightly. Her eyes were wide with the horror of what she had witnessed as he drew her final breaths. She was staring directly at John as if she were calling out for help from him.

John bowed his head and prayed for the girl's soul, then made the sign of the cross to protect himself from such evil. He then stood and began to leave the room as he noticed that her breasts had turned black and begun falling off. He could bear to watch this no more and moved into the hallway. He could hear a smashing sound coming from outside as he ran into another room.

He was standing in the window and watching the man throw the baby against the wall of the home until the crying could no longer be heard. He then picked up the dead abomination and ate its body. The sounds of crunching could be heard until he finished the tainted meal. He again stood in a trance, just staring at the place where he had killed the child.

Immediately, he began screaming in pain as he stood and writhed about as though he were having a seizure. His arms were tightly flexed as every muscle seemed to be activated at that moment. His eyes had rolled back into his skull, and he wiggled about in pain for a few more moments. Immediately after this, hand began ripping through the top of his skull and peeling him in half. Arms could be seen now as the person ripped the man in half and then stepped from the guy like he was a cheap suit. Blood had begun to be absorbed by this person.

None of this made any sense until the being looked up at him. He knew this thing could see him as he was frozen. He seemed to recognize the man but could not place his face. It was as though this person was still alive and of the same age as John. Though he still could not place the guy's face. The man walked like a robot back into the house and came up the stairs. John hid behind the bed quickly and waited for the man to come into the room. He laid the shotgun across the bed in anticipation of killing this man.

Instead, the person walked past the doorway in that same robotic manner and moved up the stairs. John followed it now as the house shifted slightly and became darker. The outside world had begun shifting to the constant lightning storm as in his time. The man walked into that room and held out his hand toward the other walls that were bare. The body of the girl that had birthed the abomination along with her father formed. They were then impaled to the wall as the figure cut them open and pulled their guts out and onto the floor.

He then bowed before the girl as though he were praying for a few moments. John stood in the doorway to the room and witnessed every second. The guy then stood slightly, reached between the girl's legs, and pulled something from her. It was her womb, or so John thought, as the guy used it to make the blood patterns all around the next room. The girl held no pain in her face nor did she seem to be the same girl who had been on the floor below.

These were the souls that were sacrificed to bring evil into the world. They were the food and life force that would awaken such a being into the existence that John had come to know. Immediately, he recognized the milky look of the girl below as the girl that had also haunted his home. Her soul had been tainted and now called out from beyond.

He could not understand anything he had witnessed until the man seemed to pull the alter from the wall and attach it in the next room. The candles were then lit as the being squeezed the flesh of the womb again. Blood dripped into the cup below, and then the flesh was thrown into the closet. Whoever this being was, it was of no consequence, and it seemed to be something horrid. The man then drank the blood from the chalice and set the cup back again.

It seemed to be an inversion of the Holy Eucharist as the symbols seemed the same but different colors and motions. The sign of the cross was in reverse, along with the bowing and prayers. This being had known to do everything as a blasphemy of such a sacred cere-mony. John wished to make the understanding that this was the antichrist, but this did not seem to be so.

The man then turned and left the room, closed the door behind him, and walked right past John. The next door was closed and locked as well as the world then shifted back to what John had come to know it. The bodies upon the wall gazed down at John and followed his movements through the room and into the next. He moved to the door of the room that contained the alter and opened it. The room was exactly as before, but it seemed to be slightly different as the candles burned upon it.

The chalice was blackened with evil, and the whole room was bathed in a sickening brownish-red aura. John pulled a flair from his waistband and pulled the cap from it. He then popped it against the wall and the sparks began to flow. He then threw it into the closet where he had once hidden. The walls seemed to do nothing at that moment until a slight flame had begun. He then threw another into the same area. This was repeated until the room had lit aflame with four separate flairs.

The flames shot higher and higher until they had engulfed the room. John ran into the next room and bashed the handle off with the shotgun. The flames now shot into the room toward the bodies. He did not stay to watch this anymore and began moving to the lower level. Then he lit another flair and tossed it onto the bed in that room, which began burning the body of the girl. He repeated this with two other rooms on this level before exiting the house.

Outside, he could see the flames jumping through the windows and wafting in the wind of the storm. John did not waste time as he rushed to the sheriff's car and started the engine. He turned for a moment to back up, only to see the long-armed man standing there. He was blocking John's path as the gas pedal was pressed, and the car sped backward until it struck the man.

John immediately knew that this was the father who had been complicit in the defilement of his own daughter. It was from him that this being had been born into the world in such a despicable manner. The man flew back into the trees as John drove the car and hammered the gas. He drove at an increasing speed until he pulled the emergency brake and slid onto the main road.

Gravel and dust followed for a moment as the world shifted back to how it was normally. He did not waste time as he sped down the road and back toward town.

10

J ohn left the squad car in the parking lot of the sheriff's office
again, then ran to his truck and sped off. The squealing of tires
could be heard throughout the night as he rushed back to his
motel and entered the room again. He immediately ran into the bathroom, only to throw up in the toilet. The bile was blackened as
though this evil had begun to affect his physical self also. He moved
to flush the toilet but was overcome with more bile.

He threw up again to reveal progressively more black substance
leaving him. Knocking began from the door to the room as he turned
and sat in the doorway to the bathroom. The knocking grew louder
and louder until it suddenly ceased. John had no other thoughts in
his mind other than what had happened at that place. He could not
understand why he had been compelled to watch such mind-altering
events.

The sickness that had welled up in that family seemed to be all-
consuming until they had been overcome by something awful. John
could hear a key slide into the lock of the door, and then the door
opened. A man rushed into the room and stood before him as John
began to fade to unconsciousness. The last thing he could feel was his
body pulling up and through the motel room.

The feeling of three men grasping his hands, back and legs was present until he was placed in a seat. John could see nothing now as it all faded to black, and he passed out. Images of torment and pain had been brought into his mind until he awoke again. This time, he was in an interrogation room that he could not recognize. The faint image of a pale and clammy-skinned man came into view.

"Mr. Dorsett, how are you?"

John gave no response to this question.

"You cannot simply leave an investigation like that and not expect us to find you. Do you know how many resources have been wasted on finding you? Then I receive a call from the sheriff of this city that you are trying to kill a poor family and burn their house down. You attempted to sexually assault their daughter and killed their son. Does this sound familiar?"

John just stared at the agent with a confused look on his face.

"Fuck you, freak! I did nothing of the kind. Get me out of this room and leave me alone!"

"Come now, Mr. Dorsett. You are a danger to others. I cannot let you go, and you know that."

"I won't answer any of your questions, and I want to know where my family are."

The agent held a slightly amused look.

"I don't know what you're meaning. There is nothing that we know about any family."

"My ex-wife called me on the phone, and I know it was you!"

The agent leaned forward and placed his arms on the table. His fingers were interlocked as he looked deep into John Dorsett's eyes.

"Make no mistake, Mr. Dorsett. There is no one that we know from your life. We are simply trying to solve the questions we have about your...case."

"You can't lie to me! What have you done to them?"

The agent turned to another and whispered something to him. That agent then approached John and stuck a needle into his neck. The expression of pain took John's face over as the substance was injected into him.

"What the hell was that? You can't just inject me with something! What the hell was that?"

The sound of a loud clicking could be heard as John passed from consciousness once more. This time, there were no sensations of feeling from his body. John had successfully passed into a dream-like state inhabited with darkness. He could not imagine or see anything within this state of being, and no dreams emerged. It was as if he were lying on the ground in this darkness and seemed unable to know where he was.

The ground was cold and harder than anything he had felt before. The world slowly came into view as John sat up from his place on the ground. He was now in a small, concrete and metal room. Nothing in his world could give him context for where he found himself now. He was not shackled to the ground, nor was he inhibited from getting up, but his body resisted the motion to stand.

If this was a jail cell, it was unlike any he had ever seen. No sound seemed to enter or exit the space, with only one door looking out onto an empty hallway. John looked about and could see no one around or any other door. It was as though he had been placed in a room and would be easily forgotten. A few moments after this, a man in a black suit moved toward the door, yet no footsteps could be heard. The man's face was hidden by the brim of his hat, placing a tinge of fear within John's mind.

He moved from the door as he waited for the man to open the door, but nothing happened. Instead, he turned to look, and the man was standing in the middle of the room.

"Mr. Dorsett, how are you feeling this morning? I trust that you had meaningful rest."

John didn't react with any other emotion other than pure shock. How did this guy get into the room without the door opening? Nothing could explain this in the least, not even the guy knowing his name, but John had never seen this man at any time.

"I know that you have made friends within the town of Fairmont, but no one will be coming for you. We will decide when you will be free. We all know what you are attempting to do, and it will never work. You cannot stop what we have begun."

John still stood in a defiant silence.

"We know that you visited the church and were instructed to do what you needed to do, but that does not matter. Your god cannot save you from us. We are everything in this world. You will fall in line like everyone else, given enough time. More importantly, you are not here. You're still asleep in your motel, and you have not left in two days. This is our power. Fear it or die"

With those words, John awoke in the same bed he had been sleeping in the Super 8 motel. Nothing had changed, nor was there anyone else in the room. John simply sighed and rubbed his eyes, trying to comprehend what the hell had just happened. Instead of lingering in the room, he simply washed his face and grabbed his keys from the nightstand. John had to meet with the sheriff and explain what had happened, but he was unsure how.

If they had known about his movements in such detail, then surely the sheriff would have fallen victim to their interrogation. He could not be sure, but John would make the effort to find his friend. He knew the plan now, and he had no other choice but could not allow the sheriff to pay for his crusade. This was all a part of the plan, but not if another man would be killed or imprisoned for John's mistakes.

With one motion, John entered the cab of his truck and left the parking lot. Though his truck was outdated, he drove through town while trying to blend into the surrounding vehicles. He feared it would stick out like a sore thumb against the other more stylized cars around him. He took a left at the corner and then drove the short distance to the next street.

He stopped his truck at the next light and looked around the area for a moment. Just then, he noticed an odd-looking man staring at him from the sidewalk. The guy seemed out of it, but looking right at John in some way. He turned his head back to the light and tried to ignore it until the man began muttering something. John was too far away to hear what the man was saying but close enough to understand that the guy was muttering. Just as John looked back to his left, he saw him walking toward John's truck. The light then changed green, and John hammered the gas pedal slightly.

His truck took off and pulled away from the crazy guy before he could get too close. The area seemed different from the days prior as people had lost their focus on anything outside of what they were doing. Normally there would be several people just walking and looking around, but everyone seemed to be looking forward. It was as though something had taken over the town and brainwashed or intimidated everyone. The whole air throughout Fairmont seemed to be heavier and darker than normal. It was as though someone had put a darkened lens over the world.

John tried to pay it no attention, but it was stark enough to continuously notice. That was until John pulled into the sheriff's office parking lot. He was now more focused on reaching the sheriff rather than those around him. Instead, he moved quickly into the office and approached the front desk.

"May I help you, sir?"

"Yes, I'm looking for the sheriff. Is he in his office?"

"I am sorry, sir, but the sheriff is out on a call right now."

"Can you tell me where? I was supposed to meet with him today, but..."

"Sir, the sheriff is not in his office. He had to go on a call and cannot talk to you right now."

"Can I wait for him?"

"I am sorry, sir. I don't think you should be waiting for him. He will be gone for a long time. We are closing up the office soon."

John knew this was suspicious but also knew that he couldn't do anything at this moment. Instead, he exited the office and returned to his truck. He immediately looked up to see the sheriff's car sitting in its parking spot. This was the confirmation that John needed most of all to know that the sheriff was in danger. He now knew the agents had caught up to him and were checking in just as the sheriff had told him. How could they know about this stuff in Fairmont of all places?

John pulled his truck around the back to the station and backed into a side alley to wait out the office closing. He kept his eyes trained on the station while looking around occasionally so no one would sneak up on him. The last of the day had given way to night as John continued to wait for the deputies to leave the office. It seemed that time passed slower than normal, but John would not abandon his friend.

After all, the sheriff had helped him from the beginning and was the only one to tell John what was happening. He might have been powerless to stop the events in '93, but he was trying to change that now. He shouldn't have to suffer for John returning to end this shit. Sheriff Barkley had to be inside or being held somewhere nearby. The one thing that John knew about these agents is that they moved together like one mind. This made them predictable in every sense of the word.

Just as this thought passed through his mind, the front office was closed with the female sheriff's deputy manning the desk emerged. She walked down to the back of the building, entered her normal car, and then drove away. John wasn't sure how to enter the building without others seeing, but he knew that there was a door in the alley on the other side. Surely, a window or door on that side would be open.

John placed a hockey mask over his face and pulled the hood of his coat over the back of his head. He then grabbed his crowbar and walked toward the building. He was worried that a small group might be left in the building to act as dispatch, but nothing had indicated that when he visited the sheriff the previous day.

John walked around the back of the building and to the alley but could not see any door or window on that side. Instead, he noticed that the back door to the building had a weakened handle that could easily be broken. He jammed the flat end of the crowbar under the edge of the handle and began to pry. He put as much pressure as he could under the edge, but then changed to short and forceful bursts of prying. The knob gave way under the pressure and split apart. There was only one loud pop as the mechanism had broken enough for John to push the other side of the handle off. He then popped the back of the locking mechanism and pulled it away from the frame.

This was an immediate method of accessing the building's back offices, which were now dark. The place seemed eerie in every sense of the word as silence overtook him. There were no sounds whatsoever within the dormant structure now. Everyone had left for the night and just left their work lying around their desks. The only sound now was the creaking of the building as it settled in the cool night air. John moved quickly and quietly through the building and to the sheriff's office in the lobby.

The door to that office was locked, but not very well, as John simply had to jiggle the knob back and forth rapidly until the door opened. Luckily, someone had only partially locked the door, with the lock snapping back to allow entry. The office was dark like the rest of the building, which was odd given that the sheriff's car was outside his very window. John immediately began looking for a clue as to where the sheriff would have been taken.

The only thing that was abundantly clear was that the sheriff had taken something from his safe in the moments that he was taken. John grabbed gloves from the box on the sheriff's desk and put them on. He looked around the safe and found nothing other than it was opened, and something was missing. He then noticed something crumpled in the back corner of the safe. It didn't seem important and could have been another piece of paper that might have been dumped into the safe accidentally.

However, John found that it was much more upon unfolding the note. It was a hastily scrawled message indicating that he had been taken to another facility that the sheriff's office maintained. The place was outside town, but John could not tell how far. Luckily, the computer on the desk was on and connected to the internet. A quick search on Yahoo revealed that the location was just near the house John and his family once inhabited. In all the years that they lived within the home, John had no idea that the facility was there, so it must have been built more recently.

The only thing left was to head there and rescue the sheriff from whoever had taken him. John left quietly through the back door, then gently shut the remainder of the door into the frame as he went. No one would be the wiser that he was there since there seemed to only be a camera in the front lobby of the building. Luckily, he had concealed his face and entered the sheriff's office. However, that could not be his worry as John jumped in his truck and turned the key.

A short drive behind the buildings in that location and toward the other road, he was free from the area and heading out of town. A tinge of anger mixed with fear rose within his chest as John contemplated his next course of action. His conclusion, however, would be to park at his house and then head through the woods to the facility. It was a dangerous prospect since the woods were infested with those horrid beings, but this was a lessened worry at this time. There was little time now as John pressed firmly on the gas pedal and listened to that modified 351 roar to life.

Time seemed to pass slowly as John peeled into the driveway of his now abandoned home. He had never visited the place since the last events of his time there. It went well beyond the days he had described to the agents in the interrogation room. He longed to see the end to this and now felt some sense of accomplishment for all he had done, but this was far from over. John did a sign of the cross which connected his forehead, solar plexus, and both shoulders.

He pulled his gun from the glove compartment and exited the truck. A quick tucking on his pants would hide the pistol from anyone who might see it. There were no words now as he moved toward the edge of the woods and lit his flashlight. He was now presented with a darkness that seemed to be all-consuming. The trees stood as an eerie reminder of what might be lurking all around him as he began entering the brush of the forest. He moved quickly and as quietly as he could at first, but was quickly met with strange shadows that moved all around him. The location of the building would be coming up quickly were it not for the fact that he would have to creep around these beings.

John pressed his back to the trees and shimmied around them until he could jump to the next. He pressed his feet onto the tops of the roots when he landed and then slid to the ground. This process was followed until he could no longer detect the shadows around him. That was until he came upon an embankment that separated him from the final stretch. There was a small creek at the bottom, which was no deeper than his ankles. John slid down to it and stepped across to the other bank.

It took all he had to jump up and grasp a root hanging from the ground above. He used it to pull and walk his way to the top of that embankment. Then, with a quick slide, he was able to get back to his feet and take the last portion of the travel quickly. He came upon the building with a row of bushes that separated the structure from the woods with a fence to climb. John moved into the bushes quietly and began peering around the area to find anyone guarding the property.

No one revealed themselves, but he thought he could see something on the rooftop of the building. A sign toward the entrance indicated that this was sheriff's office storage, but no other information could be read. John did the prudent measure and used a tree beside the fence to climb up and then scale over. The last portion of the climb was little more than a slight rattle of the fence as he grasped the top briefly then dropped to the lower bank and rolled down.

The momentum of the fall ensured that he had enough speed to press against the building in the dark. Hopefully, the shadows would conceal him in this place and allow for an easy entrance.

11

John crept to the entrance of the building and peered in through the window. He could see the sheriff tied to a chair. The rest of the room held several agents in their usual black suits and fedoras. There was little chance that he could overtake all of them, but he had little choice. John quietly entered the building and snuck behind an agent who lingered in the front room. John pulled his KA-BAR from his boot and then moved in for the kill. He snuck up to the agent and then stood quickly as he placed his hand over the agent's mouth and slid the blade through his flesh. He cut deep immediately with a puncture, then a sliding motion which freed the blade from the flesh.

There was nothing that the agent could say as he slowly slipped from reality, and John placed his body on the couch in front of them. He immediately stood staring at the dying agent and wondered why he had decided on such a messy move. There was little doubt that this would lead to someone finding the body, but he didn't care. An ever-increasing feeling of rage had taken him over at the moment as he channeled all the pain of those memories into that man. John put the thought out of his mind and remembered the mission objective as he moved to a side wall and peered into the main storage room.

The rest of the agents were interrogating the sheriff and had formed a circle around the main agent, who was clearly becoming frustrated with Sheriff Barkley. John looked around for anything to conceal him besides the few racks of items just beyond the doorway. He rushed in and rolled under a table as quietly as he could while jamming himself into his shadow. One agent looked about momentarily then refocused on the interrogation again.

There was no other option after getting to the point that he had. John knew that this would end in a blood bath and a hail of gunfire. He had nothing other than his pistol and some extra ammo. John looked around for anything useful, but only saw a pack of Pepsi sitting sealed on the ground beside the table. He grasped one of the drinks, shook it, and then threw it at the light above the agents. The lights shattered and sent Pepsi raining down atop the agents as he pulled his sidearm and began killing. He ran forward in the commotion and fired a round through the back of the nearest agent's head.

He then smashed the bottom of the handle into the face of the agent in front of him and stabbed with his KA-BAR through the chest. He had no time to witness the agent going limp and falling to the ground as he turned and planted the agent to his left through the side of his chest. John's 357 shifted to the next bullet as he pulled the trigger again and leveled a shot through the interrogator's chest. John then slid behind the sheriff and cut the zip ties that held his hands together. He then rose with his knife drawn back and began repeatedly jamming the blade into the agent directly in front of him.

He must have stabbed the agent three or four times as blood began pouring from the body and onto John's hand and knife. Flashlights were being shown all around as he heard the sheriff tackle another agent and begin shooting him. John kicked the legs out from under the last agent near him, then put his revolver to the back of the man's head and executed him immediately. The sheriff had taken care of the last two men as John recovered from the fight and stood breathing in the dark space. The sheriff approached him and thanked John.

"I thought they were going to kill me anytime. Thanks for coming for me. I wasn't sure if anyone would be willing to fight these fucking freaks. I also thought that these guys were immortal or something. They definitely look weird, to say the least. You good, John?"

John nodded, then lit his flashlight.

Both men had no idea what was coming next as a loud screeching sound rang out from above the building, with John and the sheriff struggling to leave. He stayed back for a moment as the sheriff rushed to the fence and scaled it quickly. John turned to see the agents getting back up with the first that he had killed, walking toward him from the dim light and pulling his gun. John panicked, dashed for the fence-line, and scaled it with the sheriff's help. Both men dashed into the forest and hungering darkness. They had managed to get out of sight before the agents left the building to look around.

Both men moved silently and as quickly as they could until they reached the creek and slid down into the raving around it. The sheriff remained for a moment as John scaled the other side. Both men waited as they caught their breath for a moment. No lights could be seen at that moment other than flashes coming from the other side of the wooded area. The sheriff turned and scaled to the same position that John had taken, and both men left for John's truck.

The movement through the forest was treacherous, to say the least, as both men encountered the shifting shadows once more. They seemed to be standing motionless in the dark and without any eyes that could indicate where they were looking. John had no idea how it was that they would be seeing in the dark, but they struggled to sneak through the forest again. No shadow figure seemed to even notice them or make a movement in any direction. They stood motionless in the dark and seemed to be waiting for something.

John reached the last area of the wood and pulled the sheriff out into the yard surrounding the house. John could see his truck still parked in the driveway as both men caught their breath once more.

"Damn! What the hell were those things?"

"I don't know, but the agents came back to life. I know I nearly decapitated the first agent that I encountered in the waiting room. How the hell did they come back to life? What are they?"

"I don't know, but they have been around these parts before. I'm pretty sure that the thing that I heard on the roof was the one doing the screeching. Some kind of bird or something, maybe?"

"I saw it briefly when I approached the building to rescue you, but I couldn't make out what it was."

"Doesn't matter now. We need to get the hell out of here, but we have to lay low for a moment."

John motioned to the sheriff toward and outbuilding on the edge of the yard.

"Come on, we can rest in there."

John pulled the door open as the sheriff quickly moved into the structure, and then both men hid in darkness. The sheriff looked around to ensure they were safe within the building, then turned his light off.

"So what happened with your family, and why did you leave this house?"

John looked out the window and toward the entrance to the property for a moment.

"This is a hard question to answer. It was a lot of factors that led me to abandon the place. My family was all I had in those final days, and I would not have been here today had it not been for them. My wife, Jeanette, and I had issues and continued to have issues for another several years after the first hauntings that had happened. Those damned beings kept coming back to the house over and over but didn't seem to desire to enter the home again. That girl would just stand at the back door and knock three times, then stare at the door for a long time."

I stood there in the dark some nights and listened for her. I was not able to share the bed with my wife due to issues that we were having, but I missed her company. She had given me three lovely children, and I could not do anything to repay her for her dedication to our family and me. I just know that I could not stop these beings no matter what I had tried over the years. I tried everything I could find in library books, but nothing would stop those things from appearing.

My basement would always hold that long-armed bastard while

that girl would knock on the back door, and it was that way for a long time. Then, one night, I heard Jeanette whispering into the darkness until I would come to her and ask what was going on. She would be just standing in front of the basement door and whispering. Eventually, our children would have horrible night terrors and scream out in the early morning hours. Jeanette would remember none of this and would ridicule me for always being tired and short-tempered.

I was the only one witnessing and hearing these things at night, but the rest seemed to only be affected by visions and dreams I was not. I spent countless nights holding my children until they would calm themselves and go back to sleep. Jeanette and I would always fight about it when the kids weren't around. Though I was sure that the kids would know that something had happened.

Eventually, I would sleep all night and notice anything until the last two weeks that we were in the house. It all started around The third week in December of 1996. The first event was to have Jeanette try to open the back door of that little bitch, but I stopped her since I was in the living room. We came close to her getting in, but my quick actions of grabbing Jeanette and walking her back to the bedroom saved us. I never understood what would happen when the girl got in, but I was sure it would be terrible.

I just roughed it until Friday of that week as Jeanette would continue trying to open that door, but I remember this all culminated in a night terror from my daughter. You see, I had put a chair under the door in the night so that Jeanette couldn't get out of her room. I then would check on our kids, but one night, Brianna, our youngest, had a night terror and was crying. She and I talked for a moment until she was calm, but we heard a screaming sound from outside. I thought that something had happened until we looked out the window.

We say the girl who was normally on the porch at that time knocking, but now she was below Brianna's window. She was looking up at us and screaming as if she was seeing something horrible, but then her neck began to get longer. As her neck would snake upward toward us, her head would swell until her eyes bulged and her head began to separate. I pulled Brianna into my chest so that she would not haunted by that face. She had swelled to just below the window, and it was a horrifying sight. Her ghostly skin still glowed in the darkness of the night as the moon lit her.

I've never seen anything like that before or sense, but it was awful in every sense of the word. I still cannot get that image from my mind, with her lips being distended and her head splitting open. It was not something that anyone should see. I stayed strong for my family that night, took that sight into my dreams, and blocked it out until recently. Sometimes my nightmares are haunted with that fucking knocking sound, though. Now, I think that girl is gone since I burned that infested house to the ground.

"So that is what happened. They asked me about it since it was my flairs and gas that were used, but I didn't know anything."

"Yeah, I lit that fucking place up like a Roman candle. I've never been so satisfied with anything until that night."

Anyway, I remember waking on a Monday morning around 12 AM in a cold sweat and then hearing screaming in the night. That was all followed by a banging sound coming from the basement. No one in the house could hear anything except for me, and I was not going to investigate. By this time, however, I had taken to having my gun near me. I was never sure what would happen at any moment, so I wanted to be prepared. Although, I am not sure it would have done anything.

That night ended with the sounds stopping and me falling asleep, but the next two days, Jeanette and our kids would constantly complain with headaches. They would take what they could to help with the pain, but it only lessened the throbbing from what they had told me. Eventually, they all began to sleep for most of the day as well. Then, Wednesday morning, it happened. We were all asleep until that beating sound came from the back of the basement door. I ran into the hall and pushed against the door, but it wasn't enough.

The door exploded in, and that freak came rushing into the hallway as it slammed me against the wall, and began licking the side of my face. I couldn't stop it, no matter how hard I fought against it. It eventually punched the side of my head, and I lost some consciousness. The windows in the back door shattered, and the girl came strolling in. That thing ran off, but I couldn't see what was happening. She knelt in front of me and giggled as she told me my wife was his. Now I know that that thing was the father of the family that killed themselves in the other house. He took my wife into the basement, and the girl took my kids into the woods.

I remember hearing my wife screaming for help as he pulled her into the basement. Then the screaming became faint, and only the sounds of scratching across the brick in the walls of the basement could be heard. My children were crying in the night as I regained my focus and ran into the basement, but they were gone. My children had been taken and could not be found anywhere. I searched those woods for days until I couldn't do it anymore. The basement had no clear markings where a door would be opened. I still cannot explain what had happened.

I just gave up after searching for weeks and found no one, but the sound of that girl knocking and screaming in the night was a neverpresent thing. Eventually, I started having nightmares of my wife being dragged into another realm while screaming. That would turn into nightmares of her being violated by that thing, and I could not stop them. She would always look at me and beg for help for me to kill her and end her suffering, but I don't know what happened after that.

When the dreams wouldn't stop, and I couldn't rest at any point, I sealed the house and left, but I made arrangements for the structure to be paid over time. I have feared going into that home for years and have never desired to return here. My family is gone, and I don't know how to save them, but I will find a way tonight.

John began to cry as he sat in that shed and looked out over the property.

I will be the man I could not be all these years tonight. I hope my family will forgive me, but I am not leaving until this shit's done.

The feeling that he will not be leaving this place came over John as he turned and handed the sheriff the keys to his truck. I know that

I will not be leaving this place again, so I wish for you to have my truck, and I hope that it serves you well. Just get the hell out of here, and don't let these things take anyone else.

I cannot bear the thought that someone else will be haunted and have their lives destroyed over this shit anymore. I hope that I stopped the infection that overtook this land from that lake house. I hope and pray that I brought peace to this land, and may God Almighty have mercy on our souls. Thank you for all of your help, sheriff. I could never have done all of this without you, sir.

12

John charged out of the shed and to the front door of his old home. He didn't hesitate for a moment to enter the house without any backup or anyone knowing to come for him. John's mind was set on bringing peace for his family forever, no matter the cost. He only wished for his children and wife to be at peace and pass into Heaven without him if it came to it.

John closed the door behind him and began removing his weapons as they would not do good for him now anyway. He then stepped through the old home and into the kitchen then to the pantry. He remembered installing an old iron bar in the pantry and that ghosts would be harmed if they crossed or came into contact with that beam. It took some time, but he could remove the bar and move back into the living room with a leftover bottle of rum. He sat on the couch with candles lit around the space and waited.

He was poised and waiting for these freaks to come for him in the night. The time was now 10:30PM so it was only a matter of time. The only issue would be that when he destroyed the other home, then it destroyed these entities. His mind was singularly focused on that door and the hell that he would unleash upon these beings for the harm and torture of his wife and children. John's mind raced with all the events that led to this one moment as he could not escape the thought that he should have done this long ago.

John Dorsett was no longer the coward that he had become so long ago to preserve his life and stave off death. He fled and resigned his family to torment for all these years while he hid from the images of torment that he had left for them. He could not have sacrificed himself at that time, but he was ready to do so now. If he could stop this, then surely his family would finally be at peace.

Time passed as John waited on the couch and stared toward the door. His ass had become numb from sitting on the edge of the couch, but his mind was focused. He had filled his mind with all possibilities of what he would do to these beings. Yet nothing could prepare him for the moments to come. It all started with three bangs on the basement door, followed by screaming coming from the door in front of him. He simply stood and robotically opened the back door, only to come face to face with the girl he had seen so many times. She smiled a crooked and sinister smile as he stared into her eyes.

"Welcome home, John. Daddy has been keeping her busy for you all these years."

Those words filled him with so much rage that he shoved the pipe through her faced and then beat her mercilessly until her spirit screamed out in pain and vanished. He spit on the ground in front of where she had dissipated, then returned to the house. He moved in front of the basement door and placed his hand on the locking mechanism. He had no other desire at this moment other than to kill this thing and have his family returned or released.

Just then, John heard a twisted giggle from his left, only to turn and see Brianna standing on the steps. She blew him a kiss and then ran back up the stairs. He could not stop himself from turning and calling out to her.

"Brianna! Honey! Come to Daddy! I am so sorry for all these years. I should have been there for you, baby."

John reached the top landing of the stairs and turned to see Brianna hiding at the edge of the doorway. It was all that he could do to approach her without feeling shame and guilt in his heart. He began to pray to God that she would be saved from this torment and find peace in the afterlife.

"I cannot find peace, Daddy. You left us to die and never saved us. Mommy screams out for you every minute. Why did you leave us?"

This statement broke John's mind and left him on his knees at his daughter's feet. Her spirit was no different than what she was when she was alive and flesh. He just kissed her hand, then wept at her feet.

"I am so sorry, honey! I know that I was a bad Daddy, and I couldn't save you because I was scared. It isn't an excuse and I am so sorry that I left your guys and mommy. I failed you as a father and man, and I am so sorry. Please forgive me for all that I have done."

As he sat there and sobbed into his daughter's hand, the sounds of wood breaking and splintering came from below. John didn't care, nor did he hear such sounds until the loud bangs of something moving through the structure toward him started. Laughter emanated from the lower level as one foot after another could be heard on the steps. They were moving slowly and methodically. John's grief continued to overtake him until he was no longer focused.

He was a man lost to his own sadness and grief that had over-taken him. It was all the years of pain and sadness that had been held back until this moment. There was no other understanding than the pain that he held within his heart. The tears streamed down his face and onto the floor until the footsteps reached the floor he was on.

The thing rounded the corner and began lurching toward him as he noticed that Brianna had vanished. The sadness then subsided, and rage filled him. It was an anger that he had never known before. His mind was broken now, and he was only a man who desired punishment for the wicked that had taken everything from him. John stood and turned to face the being to behold the horribly disfigured being that the father had become. Its arms were long and pale, and its mouth hung open, with something dark dripping out of it. The eyes were pitch black, and there seemed to be spores growing from its face and body that spit puss and black ink into the air.

It began stepping forward with its clammy stubs slapping against the ground as there were no feet to speak of. The thing walked on stubs that looked more like fleshy pegs with puss leaking out of the pale and clammy skin. Its mouth was left grinning as it shot its arms toward where John stood. John tightened his grip on the bar that he held and readied himself for battle. He knocked one arm into the door frame and impaled the other on the floor.

He then pulled the door closed as a crushing sound could be heard, and puss sprayed from the being. It screamed in pain as a grin came over John's face. He had been taken over by the anger now, leaving no room for sadness or fear within John's heart. The being then began to laugh as it pulled its arms and ripped the flesh apart to get them free. John yelled and rushed forward as he continuously knocked away the arms. He could hear the repeated slapping of flesh against the bar he held, and the sizzling of skin.

This being was being harmed with every touch of the iron against it as he continued until he slammed the bar across the being's face over and over. He alternated ends as he sent the iron colliding with the being's flesh over and over and over. Screaming could be heard along with sizzling until the being had been backed to the middle of the stairs and almost to the bottom floor. This left John with an opportunity as he forced the bar through the stomach of the being and into the wall.

The being screamed in pain and wiggled about as John stepped back from the thing. He delighted in its pain and misery as he smiled at it. Nothing felt better than to bring pain to his tormentor and the one who has abused his wife for so long. He relished the idea of bringing a painful death to this thing at this moment as he drew his KA-BAR from his boot and implanted it into the being's head. The sizzling grew louder and louder until John was thrown from the stairs and into the hallway of the lower level. He landed with his knife in his hand still as the thing pulled the bar from its body and began lurching toward him again.

John stood and got into a fighter's stance with the knife in his right hand and feet firmly planted on the floor. He was ready to take this thing to hell with him. The being dripped with puss and writhed about like a thousand worms cut in half. It charged John, as he began stabbing the thing mercilessly until it threw him down into the basement.

John slammed against the brick wall in the basement while being dazed. He could see all around him that the basement was darker than he remembered, and only a faint light shined in the middle. John took his feet again as he felt a warm and thick liquid pouring from the back of his head. He could do nothing but continue the fight to his last breath.

The being stepped down from the last step and into the basement proper as it confronted John. They both glared at each other as they rushed forward and became entangled. John stabbed relentlessly until the thing was left writing on the ground. It was do this for a moment, then stand again. Until John stepped forward and began slicing its arms from its body.

Puss and ooze sloshed onto the basement floor in a goopy mess that seemed to slowly puddle on the floor. The smell was horrendous as John planted his knife deep into the eye of the being and shoved it further. The blade had begun to emerge from the back of the being. It fell upon the ground and writhed again until laughter emanated.

"I have your family, and I will forever. Your weak efforts cannot kill me. They will suffer at my hands for all eternity. Only you can take their place, and I will let them go, but someone has to be food for our desires. Give in to it and be taken from this world!"

The thing stood from the floor only to be joined by the apparition of the screaming girl again. They joined and held hands as they smiled and celebrated John's failure. The anger began to overwhelm John at that moment and would not stop. He became consumed by his rage and lost all mind in the face of these beings. John then yelled out as he lifted the knife above his head.

"Hear me, oh Lord! I give my life in sacrifice to save my family from the torment of these evil things! Grant them peace and rest forever more, and have mercy upon me, your hand of justice!"

With those words, John slit his wrists and sat down on the ground as the blood flowed. The beings laughed again and approached John. We will release them as agreed, but you are to become like us. We will prey upon the world and those that live here. Slowly, you will be given to him just like we gave ourselves. They have made the way for this world to be ours, and we will rule it.

John laughed loudly as he pulled a lighter from his pocket and began flicking it. Just then, the lighter flicked onto a gasoline line that ran through a tube and into a gas canister. The whole of the house exploded and erupted into flames. John was blown from the basement and into the yard as he drew his last breaths. The only sounds that could be heard were the creaking and popping of the house burning, along with John's laughter. He would die a happy man, knowing that he had saved his wife and children.

He then felt the gentle touch of three hands on him. He turned to see his wife and his three children step in front of him. They comforted him as he began to slip into death.

"You did right by us, John. I am sorry that we ever doubted you. Come with us, and we will rest."

It was said that day that anyone in the area could watch the house burn from all corners of that valley. John rose from his body and marched into the woods with his family in his arms and into peace.

Some say that you can still hear the screams of those apparitions burning within that house to this day. Though you will have to hear that along with the loud sounds of a man laughing maniacally into the night. John saved Fairmont that night and left the area with a sense of peace. He brought the evil there to its knees, but some say that the agents will never truly lose grasp of what they bring to this world.

ABOUT THE AUTHOR

Nicholas Barker debuted his work and creativity in the writing world with his first book, *Inhumanity*, which he wrote over several years while discovering what truly terrifies him. This is in addition to his second novel *Faces of Inhumanity*. Nicholas has taken his time to craft stories and poems to entertain audiences. He has deep roots within the folklore of the Blue Ridge Mountains of North Carolina and draws upon this to entertain his fans. He draws heavily from his knowledge of the supernatural and mythology to bring new worlds to life. He dreams of becoming a full-time writer and poet for all the world to enjoy through his passions.

BOOKS BY NICHOLAS BARKER

Inhumanity

Faces of Inhumanity

What Darkness Remains

AFTERWORD

Go to hangaripublishing.com to learn more about the Authors and stay up to date with their newest releases.

www.ingramcontent.com/pod-product-compliance
Lightning Source LLC
Chambersburg PA
CBHW071200120626
46546CB00006B/2355